Old Sturbridge Village Cookbook

Old Sturbridge Village Cookbook

Authentic Early American Recipes
for the Modern Kitchen

Third Edition

Edited by Debra Friedman and Jack Larkin

ThreeForks®

GUILFORD, CONNECTICUT
HELENA, MONTANA

AN IMPRINT OF THE GLOBE PEQUOT PRESS

ThreeForks®

Copyright © 1984, 1995, 2009 by Old Sturbridge Village

A ThreeForks Book
ThreeForks is a registered trademark of The Globe Pequot Press.

Design by Sheryl P. Kober
Illustrations by Cynthia Dias-Reid

Library of Congress Cataloging-in-Publication Data
Old Sturbridge Village cookbook : authentic early American recipes for the mod-
ern kitchen / edited by Debra Friedman and Jack Larkin. — 3rd ed.
      p. cm.
  Includes index.
  ISBN 978-0-7627-4929-4
  1. Cookery, American–New England style–History–19th century. I. Friedman,
Debra. II. Larkin, Jack, 1943- III. Old Sturbridge Village.

TX715.2.N48O428 2009
641.5974–dc22

                                                                2008042533

Printed in the United States of America

10 9 8 7 6 5 4 3 2 1

Contents

Acknowledgments

For over sixty years staff members at Old Sturbridge Village have been studying the foodways and cooking techniques of early New England and demonstrating them to generations of museum visitors. This third edition of the *Old Sturbridge Village Cookbook* builds on the previous versions and represents the work of many Village staff members, past and present. Debra Friedman, Director of Interpretation, and Jack Larkin, Chief Historian, have served as the Village's editors. Debra Friedman, with the assistance of Ryan Beckman, has tested additional recipes on the hearth. The previous editions were edited by Caroline Sloat, with the assistance of Linda Oakley and Anna T. Adams. Cynthia Dias-Reid created the illustrations.

Others have contributed in many ways, including those who sampled recipes as they were tested. Old Sturbridge Village extends its appreciation to all of them.

INTRODUCTION

The *Old Sturbridge Village Cookbook* gives today's readers a close look at how New England families cooked in the early 1800s. It also provides authentic recipes from early America's most popular cookbook in a form that can be reproduced in the modern kitchen.

The American Frugal Housewife

"The true economy of housekeeping is simply the art of gathering up all the fragments, so that nothing be lost." This is how Lydia Maria Child introduced *The American Frugal Housewife*, a book of recipes and forthright advice on household management first published in Boston in 1829. She wrote her book to fill a need that she found in her own experience as cook and housekeeper. Despite "the great variety of cookery books already in the market," she wrote, she "did not know of one suited to the wants of the middling class in our own country." Her perception must have been accurate, for many thousands of households bought copies of the *Frugal Housewife*, keeping it in print for the next twenty years. Some young women, who left their farm homes to work in New England's new textile factories, actually sent the book home to their mothers with their first earnings! An entire generation of New England women relied on Mrs. Child's commonsensical advice and cooked with her recipes.

One of Mrs. Child's goals was to help women manage their households efficiently, whether in the countryside or the city. She gave helpful advice on the economical use of time and materials, and on keeping rooms clean and children busy. She provided instructions on how to take care of furniture and carpets, and tips on health care and grooming. But her primary aim was to improve the standard of cooking. More than anything, Mrs. Child wanted to instruct her readers how to preserve food and prepare meals—efficiently, inexpensively, and well.

The American Frugal Housewife spoke so eloquently to the nation's households that it remains an important source for learning about hearth and home in the early years of the American republic. Mrs. Child's book is still actively in use at Old Sturbridge Village, the outdoor museum of early-nineteenth-century New England, where it guides the Village's demonstration and interpretation of cooking and domestic life.

Each year, hundreds of thousands of visitors come to the Village, in Sturbridge, Massachusetts, to watch costumed staff members cook Mrs. Child's recipes in restored early-nineteenth-century kitchens. Many of them get involved in hands-on cooking activities during their visit or in special programs. They frequently ask, "Where can I find these recipes?" and "How can I cook them at home?"

Many of the recipes provided in the *Old Sturbridge Village Cookbook* are based on the experiences of the Village staff in finding out just how the recipes in Mrs. Child's book should be prepared, and how the results should taste.

Mrs. Child wrote about the kind of cooking she knew best—hearth cooking. There was just about no alternative in her time. Cookstoves were still uncommon and

Old Sturbridge Village

A trip to Old Sturbridge Village, the largest outdoor history museum in the Northeast, is a journey through time to a rural New England town of the 1830s. Visitors are invited into more than forty original buildings, each carefully researched, restored, and brought to the museum site from towns throughout New England. These include homes, meetinghouses, a district school, country store, bank, law office, printing office, carding mill, gristmill, pottery, blacksmith shop, shoe shop, cooper shop, and an accurately reproduced sawmill.

Authentically costumed staff, called history interpreters, carry out the daily activities of an early-nineteenth-century community. Here you may wander country roads and visit with a farmer plowing fields, listen to the blacksmith's rhythmic hammering, or smell the aroma of bread baking in a fireplace oven. With four unique seasons and more than 200 acres to explore, there is always something new to see at Old Sturbridge Village.

The period of American history portrayed by Old Sturbridge Village, 1790–1840, is of major significance because it was a time in which the everyday lives of New Englanders were transformed by the rise of commerce and manufacturing, improvements in agriculture and transportation, the pulls of emigration and urbanization, and the tides of educational, political, cultural, and social change.

The Village's portrayal of the past is grounded in award-winning historical research that includes archaeology, scientific analysis of nineteenth-century objects and buildings, and painstaking study of letters, diaries, account books, and other documents.

Old Sturbridge Village is located in Sturbridge, Massachusetts, on U.S. Route 20 near the junction of the Massachusetts Turnpike (Interstate 90, exit 9) and Interstate 84, exit 2. You can learn more about the Village's exhibits and programs, and about planning your visit, at www.osv.org, or by calling (508) 347–3362.

many of them did not yet work well. Her directions call for using the fireplace, a direct and effective source of heat for cooking. Hearth cooking involves using cranes to hang pots directly over the fire, roasting meats on a spit, and cooking a variety of other dishes with the fire's glowing coals—using bake-kettles and iron trivets. Bread and pies were baked just above the hearth, as coals were heaped into the fireplace's bake oven.

Using the *Frugal Housewife*'s instructions, hearthside cooks at Old Sturbridge Village have been able to perfect these techniques. Village cooks prepared each of the book's recipes at the hearth or in the brick oven. With these results as a guide, they prepared the recipes again, this time on a modern stove. Now tested and verified, the recipes appear in this book in three ways: first, in their original form, as they appeared in Mrs. Child's and other early cookbooks; second, with hearth-cooking instructions for today's cooks; and third, as adapted for modern stove cooking.

Early New England Cookbooks

For generations, housewives in both New and old England cooked primarily from the traditional "receipts" of their mothers and grandmothers—sometimes written down, but more often strictly from memory. Toward the end of the eighteenth century, however, the publishing industry greatly expanded in America—and both men and women became increasingly interested in finding advice in print on many different subjects. Cooking was one of them.

The American Frugal Housewife was not New England's first cookbook. The earliest ones used in New England, as elsewhere in America, were English. Some were imports, and others were American editions of English works. Many of them could not have been easy for their readers to use, because they often ignored common American foodstuffs while including others rarely available on this side of the Atlantic. English cookbook authors also assumed that meals would be prepared and brought to the table by servants—something that was true for only a small minority of New England households.

As recipes were found to be appealing, however, they were gradually incorporated into versions adapted for the American market or copied by New England women for their personal recipe collections.

One of the most widely used English books was Susannah Carter's *The Frugal Housewife* and *Compleat Woman Cook*, a work popular in England that went through several American editions between 1772 and the early 1800s. Its first American printing included illustrations engraved by Paul Revere. Editions of Carter's *Frugal Housewife* after 1800 began to acknowledge the differences between English and American foodways; they featured "an appendix containing new receipts adapted to the American mode of cooking."

Another English cookbook widely republished in America was Maria Rundell's *A New System of Domestic Cookery*, with ten editions between 1807 and 1823. It went through several additional editions after it was repackaged as *The Experienced American Housekeeper or Domestic Cookery*. Yet despite the "new" version's claim that it was "adapted to the use of private families throughout the United States," its recipes still called for English ingredients that American cooks could not easily find.

The earliest genuinely American cookbook was the work of another New England cook, Amelia Simmons. Her *American Cookery* was published in 1796 in Hartford, Connecticut. We know little about her except that she described herself as an "American orphan" who learned her cookery the hard way as an often poorly treated "household help." The full title of her book doubles as its table of contents: *American Cookery* or the Art of Dressing Viands, Fish, Poultry, and Vegetables and the best modes of making pastes, puffs, pies, tarts, puddings, custards and preserves and all kinds of cakes from the imperial plumb to plain cake, adapted to this country and all grades of life. Simmons's *American Cookery* was reprinted in many different editions over the next forty years, some not even crediting Simmons as the author.

Simmons's book was successful because it was written from actual experience in a New England kitchen using ingredients that were commonly available. It included recipes for johnnycakes and flapjacks using cornmeal, for pies made with such New World vegetables as pumpkins and squash, and for gingerbread made with molasses, a syrupy sweetener ubiquitous in New England country stores and less costly than refined sugar. None of these foods were known in Old England,

but all had become standard fare for New Englanders. However, not all of Mrs. Simmons's recipes originated in a New England kitchen. Some are very similar to those in Carter's *Frugal Housewife*, suggesting that she used it and borrowed a few recipes.

Carter's *Frugal Housewife*, Rundell's *Domestic Cookery*, and Simmons's *American Cookery* were all available in various editions when Mrs. Child began to write, although she seems to have been unaware of Susannah Carter's book when she titled her own work *The Frugal Housewife*. In her second edition she noted that "it became necessary to change the title" to include the word American "because there is an English work of the same name, not adapted to the wants of this country."

What Americans wanted, Mrs. Child wrote, was "information . . . of a common kind . . . such as the majority of young housekeepers do not possess and such as they cannot obtain from cookery books." It was designed to appeal to women who, like herself, had to stretch limited resources into an appearance of elegance and plenty. Close to one-third of the book consisted of down-to-earth advice about running a household—keeping things clean, curing simple ailments, purchasing economically, and raising children. A true daughter of New England, she opposed allowing children to "romp away" all their time at play; even off the farm they could be given simple household chores that would teach them useful skills as well as discipline and self-control.

At the center of the book was a wide range of down-to-earth recipes, grouped under the headings "Common

Cooking," "Vegetables," "Herbs," "Puddings," "Common Pies," "Common Cakes," "Bread, Yeast, &c." and "Preserves, &c." The *Old Sturbridge Village Cookbook* follows this original order, while adding a separate section on "Soups" which brings these recipes together.

When she wrote her cookbook in 1829, Mrs. Child was twenty-seven years old. Born Lydia Maria Francis, she lived until she was twelve with her parents in Medford, just outside Boston, where her father was a baker. After her mother died in 1814, her father "broke up housekeeping," as they said at the time, sending young Maria to live with her married sister, Mary Francis Preston, in Norridgewock, Maine. Maria helped Mary with housekeeping, with the new babies as they came along, and with feeding and entertaining many visitors. Mary Preston's husband was a lawyer, and the county seat of Norridgewock often bustled with lawyers who visited at night and sometimes boarded for weeks at a time, greatly adding to the work of the household. Maria attended school and read voraciously, but she also received a practical education in household management.

In her late teens, Maria left her sister's home to become a teacher in a district school in another town in Maine. She returned to Massachusetts when her newly married older brother, Unitarian minister Convers Francis, invited her to join his household in Watertown. Always intent on keeping busy, she opened a school for girls and began to write. Her first book, *Hobomok*, a novel about New England in the seventeenth century, was published in 1824 and was successful enough that in the following year she followed it with *The Rebels*, a story of the American Revolution. In 1826 she began *The Juvenile Miscellany*, the nation's first periodical for young people. By her early twenties, she was an established teacher and becoming well known as a writer. She was also being courted by an idealistic young lawyer, David Lee Child.

Soon after Maria and the charming but impractical David were married in October of 1828, it became apparent that the income from her writing was vital for their support. Maria turned from fiction to a more practical, and she hoped more lucrative, subject. Drawing on her experience as a domestic manager and cook, she hit upon the idea of a new American cookbook and set about writing it. But then she had to get it published. Her manuscript was rejected by a number of publishing houses, she wrote, "on account of the variety of cookbooks already on the market." But she persevered, and finally convinced a pair of Boston publishers, Marsh & Capen, and Carter & Hendee, to taken on the project. It was a successful gamble for them. By 1850 the cookbook had gone through thirty-two editions.

She continued to edit *The Juvenile Miscellany* and went on to write other books of advice that drew on her experience both educational and domestic: *The Mother's Book*, *The Girls' Own Book*, and *The Family Nurse*. However, Mrs. Child became a controversial figure when she emerged as an advocate for the antislavery movement in the mid-1830s. She lost many friends, her periodical failed as subscribers canceled, and *The Family Nurse* found few readers. After 1840 she devoted most of her writing to the abolitionist cause; in 1865 she wrote her last book of advice, *The Freedmen's Book*, directed at newly freed slaves. Still, her cookbook remained in wide use in American kitchens, literally making "Mrs. Child" a household word.

Eventually, of course, *The American Frugal Housewife* was superseded by newer cookbooks. One was *The New England Economical Housekeeper* of 1845, published in Worcester, Massachusetts. Esther Allen Howland, its author, both admired Mrs. Child's book and copied from it. She paraphrased its title, substituting "New England" for "American," "Economical" for "Frugal," and "Housekeeper" for "Housewife." Mrs. Howland also included a number of Mrs. Child's recipes—as usual, without giving credit. But most of what she provided was new, reflecting the passage of twenty years and the evolution of cooking techniques, particularly those that involved the now widely used cookstove. Mrs. Howland's husband was a prominent bookseller in Worcester, who must have been pleased with the public response to his wife's book. Its first edition of 1,500 copies sold out in fifteen weeks, and new editions followed in rapid succession.

Fifty years later, in 1895, Mrs. Child's book surfaced again, but in a curious disguise. By then, the cookbooks of the years before the Civil War had long fallen out of use. New England's most popular cookbook near the turn of the century was probably the indomitable Fannie Farmer's *Boston Cooking School Cook Book*. But a group of ladies in Deerfield, Massachusetts, decided to create an "old-fashioned" cookbook as a fund-raising project for their church. They published *The Pocumtuc Housewife*, "a guide to domestic cookery as practiced in the Connecticut Valley," claiming that it was based on "original sources" dating from 1805. But in fact their book borrowed most of its content from *The American Frugal Housewife*, while adding some recipes and antiquarian notes of their own. Although purchasers of this little volume have probably not known much about its actual origins, it has remained in print, benefiting the Parish Guild of the First Church of Deerfield, Massachusetts. Happily, *The American Frugal Housewife* is itself now back in print. Since the 1990s, a facsimile of the twelfth edition of 1832 has been published by Applewood Books in association with Old Sturbridge Village.

Early cookbooks gave directions in a style that to modern eyes seems vague and unclear. They often did not bother with specific amounts and left many steps of the cooking process to be filled in by the reader. Even then, this vagueness could be disastrous for beginning cooks. In her autobiography, Mary Livermore recalled one of her first cooking experiences as a minister's young bride. She was attempting to follow her cookbook's directions for making a fish chowder. However, the recipe was not sized for a household of two. It called for vast amounts of ingredients—far too much as it turned out—and for others that she was completely lacking. In her inexperience, she did her best to substitute and resize the ingredients, and hung the chowder to cook in a kettle over the fire. She cooked it twice as long as the cookbook directed, but to no avail—it was uncooked on top, burned on the bottom, and completely inedible throughout. "After dark that night," she wrote, "the masculine head of the house quietly buried it in a corner of the garden, that the incompetence of his wife, as a cook, might never be discovered and bruited about."[1] *The Old Sturbridge Village Cookbook* is designed to avoid such painful episodes.

This cookbook presents most of the recipes from *The American Frugal Housewife*, along with some other early ones that have been successfully prepared at Old Sturbridge Village. It is organized along the lines of the original, but some of the recipes from The *Frugal Housewife* have been omitted; they call for ingredients that are no longer commonly available or likely to appear on an American family's table today. Thus no recipes for souse, tripe, pigeon, or roast pig have been included. Few cooks today need to know how to ascertain the age of a pigeon before deciding whether to pot it, roast it, or stew it. It also seems unlikely that they would want to know that a roasting pig is half done "when the eyes drop out," or would desire directions for cooking a calf's head with the windpipe attached.

The cookbook also omits some common dishes. Early English and American cooks usually made puddings in cloth bags submerged in boiling water, and Mrs. Child provided a variety of such recipes. Over the years these directions have proved very difficult to follow. Even experienced hearth cooks at the Village have needed repeated experiments to produce an edible result. Boiled puddings are still cooked as part of historical demonstrations at the museum, but they are not practical for modern kitchens.

Leaving out recipes like these left room to include a number that have been popular with Village staff and those who have participated in the museum's hearth-cooking classes and programs.

New England Cooking

It was said of early-nineteenth-century New England that the region's "food may well be called substantial and the variety and quantity are enough to denote a land of plentiful supply."[2] A successful farmer, Calvin Plimpton of Easton, Massachusetts, spoke for many New Englanders when he wrote of wanting "meat or its equivalent to be served three times a day." To have such hearty fare available throughout the year, each fall he would lay by "a part of a sheep, beef and a barrel of oysters."[3] In the countryside, most New England families had access to food from their own fields and barns or their neighbors' farms.

Families in the cities might count on relatives in the countryside for an occasional parcel of meat or cheese, but generally they had to rely on the marketplace. For Bostonians, the area around Fanueil Hall had long been the principal food market. After the huge Quincy Market was built in 1825, its granite halls were filled every day with men and women shopping for meat, dairy, fruit, and vegetables.

When a New England farmer took over the operation of the family farm from his aging parents, he sometimes signed a bond for their support, promising to provide them with food in specific quantities and varieties. An elderly couple in Vermont were guaranteed "a healthy merchantable fat hog, weighing 300 pounds, three hundred pounds of good beef, half a barrel of Mackerel No. 2, also the milk and calves of three good cows." The farm was also to provide them with "rye and Indian [corn], meal potatoes, cyder apples, garden sauce of all kinds and also fruit of all kinds in their season." In addition, there were foodstuffs from the store: "five bushels of wheat, one pound of green tea, two pounds of bohea tea and ginger, alspice and pepper of each one pound, ten pounds of brown sugar, two pounds of loaf sugar, one gallon of molasses, one of West India rum and two gallons of cider brandy," as well as an unspecified quantity of salt.[4]

Characteristic of the dietary patterns of its time and place, *The American Frugal Housewife* gave meat and fish a prominent a place among its recipes. Its section devoted to the preparation of meat, poultry, and fish is simply titled "Common Cooking." These recipes include roasting, broiling, and stewing various cuts of beef, veal, mutton, lamb, pork, and poultry, making hashes and meat pies, and preparing several different kinds of fish. For city families, Mrs. Child recommended careful purchasing at the market. Cuts that could provide more than one meal were the most economical, she maintained, even if not always the cheapest by the pound. Writing in a world without refrigeration, she cautioned her readers to pay careful attention to the condition of their meat. Whether they stored it fresh in the coolest

possible place in the house, or kept it in brine, they needed to check it frequently to prevent spoilage.

The New England day traditionally began with breakfast, described by more than one observer as "no evanescent thing." In the country "breakfast is held at an early hour and often by sunrise."[5] The hour was not so early, however, that a lot of cooking couldn't take place, including the baking of fresh bread. Several of the *Frugal Housewife*'s bread recipes include "setting a sponge"— mixing a thin batter with yeast in the evening to allow the bread to rise overnight in cold weather. The bread was allowed to rise a second time in the early morning while the brick oven took two hours to preheat.

Mrs. Child made one specific—and to us, surprising—menu suggestion for breakfast: fish cakes. "There is no way of preparing salt fish for breakfast so nice," she wrote, "as to roll it up in little balls, after it is mixed with mashed potatoes; dip it into egg and fry it brown." In the prosperous household of Judge Joseph Lyman of Northampton, Massachusetts, his daughter Ann Jean recalled that "the breakfast was always simple but abundant, tea and coffee, broiled fish or steak, bread and some kind of pudding for the children to be eaten with milk or cream."[6] Some New Englanders ate their breakfast meat cold. "Boiled beef, when thoroughly done," wrote Sarah Josepha Hale, in her cookbook of 1839, "is excellent to eat cold, as a relish for breakfast. The slices should be cut even and very thin."[7] The most bountiful breakfasts seem to have been prodigious in size, sometimes consisting of "ham, beef, sausages or pork, as well as bread, butter, boiled potatoes, pies, coffee and cider."[8] The aromas of frying meat, fresh bread, and coffee must have brought many a hardworking farmer in from barn chores for breakfast.

Dinner was the major meal of the day, served at 1:00 p.m. for country families and an hour later in the city. Contrary to later New England tradition, it was the Sunday noon meal that was the exception to the rule of a hot dinner with meat and potatoes followed by some kind of pudding. Many devout families did not do any heavy cooking on the Sabbath, and took their meals warmed over. If they lived at a distance from the meetinghouse, they could not return home between the morning and afternoon services and had a cold repast while sitting in the pews.

In the Lyman household, dinner was "always a joint roast or boiled with plenty of vegetables and few condiments, for Mother thought them unwholesome, good bread and butter and a plain pudding or pie."[9] In the Braintree home of former President John Adams, Josiah Quincy remembered "the modest dinners at the

President's to which I brought a schoolboy's appetite." He recalled years later that "the pudding generally composed of boiled cornmeal always constituted the first course. This was the custom of the time, it being thought desirable to take the edge off one's hunger before reaching the joint."[10] Other families reversed the order, serving "hasty pudding" as a dessert at the end of the meal, with butter and molasses.

The best-remembered dinner of the New England year was the Thanksgiving meal, which could last as long as two hours while a great abundance of food made its way to the table. As Edward Everett Hale described it in *A New England Boyhood*, "You began with your chicken pie and your roast turkey. You ate as much as you could, and you then ate what you could of mince pie, squash pie, Marlborough pie, cranberry tart and plum pudding. Then you went to work on the fruits as you could. The use of dried fruits at the table was much more frequent in those days than in these. Dates, prunes, raisins, figs and nuts held a much more prominent place in a handsome dessert."[11] New Englanders agreed, Catharine Sedgwick wrote, that the Thanksgiving feast was a "noble dinner" where those around the table should be "as happy as possible remembering who it is that has given us all these good things."[12]

For the most fashionable households in urban places, the dinner hour was already beginning to shift to the evening, the pattern that American families generally follow today. But for the great majority of families in the early nineteenth century, the last meal of the day was

called "tea," taken between 5:00 and 6:00 p.m. Belying its name, it was a substantial repast. Bread and butter, sometimes freshly made biscuits, assorted cakes, relishes, and even meats were on the menu. If available, fresh fruits, like strawberries, were served; if not, apple sauce, baked apples, other preserves, and pickles made their appearance along with "an abundant supply of tea and coffee, with thin slices of bread and butter doubled, sponge cake made by the daughters before breakfast and thin slices of cold tongue or ham."[13] Neighbors were often invited over to take tea, since it came at the end of the day's work. Women's sewing societies, which met in the afternoons at members' homes, generally sewed for several hours, socialized over tea, with "many accompaniments . . . bread, buttered, cheese and nut cakes or sponge cake . . . ," and then adjourned.[14]

One cookbook recommended that "common gingerbread and several varieties of the cheap and simple cakes are much better as a part of the evening meal than hot biscuits or even a full supper of cold bread and butter in the winter season, when butter is too heavily salt [for preservation] to be healthful."[15] Teatime was often a hungry time, and in one reminiscence, the family would make "sad havoc among the flapjacks, gingerbread and plumb cakes."[16] In another family "great kettles full of hasty pudding were easily disposed of as 'pudding and milk' and too little remained to serve as fried pudding at breakfast."[17]

In the most prosperous families, later evening repasts, usually called "suppers," were often elaborate.

If there were evening callers by invitation or by chance, a tray of fancy cakes might be passed around, accompanied by glasses of wine or brandy. Evening parties—an "oyster supper" was a fashionable favorite—had special menus. "Such parties are very common in private families of fashionable standing," noted Robert Roberts, in *The House Servant's Directory*. Roberts provided directions for special table settings for eating a selection of hot and cold foods, as well as glasses for wine, champagne, and cold water. He noted also that cards might well be played before the supper was served.[18] At the eightieth birthday party for John Quincy Adams—John Adams's son and a former President himself—dancing preceded a "pretty supper, with ices and champagne."[19] And at the end of a long day of eating and drinking, some New Englanders confessed to having a glass of brandy or gin with hot water to aid digestion and a good night's sleep.

Mrs. Child presented her recipes without anecdotal descriptions, but some have interesting stories attached to them. Election Cake, sweetened bread made with yeast, was a dish that figured prominently in New Englanders' childhood memories. In Massachusetts, it was made to mark the springtime election of the governor, and "Old Election, 'Lection Day as we call it" was mourned as a "lost holiday" by the end of the nineteenth century. "It came at the most delightful season, the last of May [when] lilacs and tulips were in bloom." As the militia mustered ceremonially on the green, children looked forward to slices of the Election Cake that their mothers had made for the occasion. "It was nothing but a kind of sweetened

Breakfast

– 1 –	– 2 –
Mince Meat or Sliced Cold Beef	Apple Pie
Fried Cucumbers	Codfish Cakes
Fried Potatoes	Toast, Butter
Three-Grain Bread, Butter	Hasty Pudding, Fried in Slices, with Molasses
Tea, Coffee	Tea, Coffee

Tea

"The common gingerbread and several varieties of the cheap and simple cakes . . ."

Doughnuts

Flapjacks

Sliced Ham

Potted Cheese

Bread and Butter

Refreshments for the Militia

"After the oration came another national salute, thirteen guns, one for each of the original states . . . and then an attack upon the bread and cheese and rum punch provided by the committee."

–Francis M. Thompson, *History of Greenfield, Shire Town of Franklin County*
(Greenfield, 1904)

Dinner

"A large joint roast or boiled with plenty of vegetables and few condiments, good bread and butter and a plain pudding or pie."

— 1 —

Roast Veal
Roast Potatoes Under the Meat
Stewed Beets
Lemon Pudding

— 2 —

Alamode Beef
Stuffing Balls
Mashed Potatoes
Pickled Beets
Rice Pudding with Fruit

— 3 —

Chicken Fricassee
Boiled Potatoes
Crookneck Squash Pudding
Parsnips
Cranberry Pie

— 4 —

Roast Pork
Broiled Potatoes
Applesauce
Turnip Sauce
Apple Pie

— 5 —

"An Economical Dinner"
Baked Beans with Pork
Indian Pudding

— 6 —

"A Very Economical Dinner"
1 lb. Sausage, Cut in Pieces
Potatoes Fried with
Onions
Squash Pie

Thanksgiving Dinner

Roast Turkey, Stuffed
Boiled Stuffed Chicken
Chicken Pie
Mashed Potatoes
Turnip Sauce, Squash, Onions
Gravy

Applesauce, Cranberry Sauce
Long Rolls
Quaking Plum Pudding with Better Sweet Sauce
Mince, Pumpkin, and Cranberry Pies
Marlborough Pudding

bread with a slice of egg and molasses on top," wrote Lucy Larcom, "but we thought it delicious."[20]

Although the apocryphal story of George Washington and the cherry tree (created by the shameless Parson Weems in 1799) had been in print for a generation, Americans of the 1830s were not eating cherry pies in the General's honor. But there was a popular recipe for Washington Cake. A version of the recipe that appeared in a New Hampshire newspaper in 1843 noted that "Washington cake was so called because it was a favorite at the table of General Washington."[21]

Implicit in *The American Frugal Housewife* are assumptions about the sources of food, methods of storage, ways of measuring, and handy substitutes in the larder that were available to the households of 170 years ago. Part of the fun of reading and interpreting the old recipes is that it helps us understand everyday life in kitchens of the past.

Food arrived at the early New England table along pathways very different from those of today. Farm families grew their own corn and rye, and occasionally their own wheat as well. Harvested grain was taken to be ground at the local mill, and each year's crop supplied both food and seed for the following one. Corn was grown primarily for bread and animal fodder. It was left in the fields until the kernels dried and hardened on the cob; the most common New England variety was called flint corn. When the corn was dry enough, the ears were picked, husked, cleaned from the cob, and taken to the gristmill to be ground into cornmeal. Sometimes a small patch of corn was picked when the ears were still small and the kernels still soft, and then boiled for eating.

Wheat flour tells its own story of the transformation of rural life. Wheat was not commonly grown in New England. Soil, climate, and diseases decreased its yield and made it a poor choice for farmers. Traditionally, New England families made bread with rye and corn, usually called "rye and Indian," reserving wheat flour, brought from New York's Hudson Valley or Pennsylvania, for special occasions. But the settlement of western New York and Ohio, improvements in road transportation, and the opening of the Erie Canal in 1825, made wheat flour less expensive and more available. By the 1820s, barrels of New York and Ohio wheat flour were appearing in New England country stores as well as on city shelves. New England cooks, with a strong taste for whiter breads and baked goods, much preferred wheat flour to the dark "rye'n Injun," and so the consumption of New England's traditional breadstuff declined sharply. (See "A Note on Flour," page 155.)

Without refrigeration or canning, families had to eat their foods, or process them for storage, in the seasons in which they grew. Beans and peas had to be shelled and dried. Other vegetables, particularly cucumbers and cabbages, could be pickled in vinegar, and flavored with herbs and spices. Pumpkins, squashes, cabbages, and onions had to be stored in dry places where they would not freeze. "See that your vegetables are neither sprouting nor decaying," Mrs. Child advised her readers. "Examine your pickles to see that they are not growing soft and tasteless." It is little wonder that root crops were grown in such abundance in the gardens of the early nineteenth century; they were by far the easiest to preserve. Stored in root cellars, potatoes, turnips, beets, and carrots could be kept for months in barrels of sand.

For meat too, the seasons of the year determined what was available and whether it was fresh or preserved. Urban markets provided supplies of fresh meat for city dwellers long before rural families could have access to them. For the most part, the farm's meat supply was determined by its traditional seasonal calendar. Cattle and hogs were butchered in the early winter, just as they stopped grazing to go on their winter fodder of hay and grain. The chilly days of late November and December gave farm families a chance to enjoy some fresh meat, and then allowed them to cut up pork and beef without risk of it spoiling before it was "salted," or stored in barrels of brine to be consumed in the ensuing year. *The American Frugal Housewife* provided directions for preparing storage barrels and making brine. Farm families smoked meat for flavor as well, particularly pork, but it had to be thoroughly salted first so that it would keep. Winter was also the time to make sausage from the scraps of meat left over from butchering.

Veal and lamb were sometimes eaten in the later part of the spring, when young animals were available. In the country, chickens, geese, and turkeys could be eaten at almost any time, since they could be killed and completely eaten before there was danger of spoilage. In city markets, however, poultry was most available

and cheapest in the late summer or fall, when the birds were large enough to withstand a journey along the roads from the country towns where they had been raised.

The records of country stores tell us that New England families ate sizable quantities of salt fish in the summer months. Fishermen brought their catches to the wharves of Cape Cod and Cape Ann in Massachusetts, where they were soaked in brine produced by the local salt works, dried on racks that covered the beaches, and barreled for sale.

Salt meat and fish posed significant challenges to the cook, since salt enhanced preservation but not flavor. Mrs. Child included extensive directions for making both salted fish and meat edible by "freshening"—thoroughly and repeatedly soaking the pieces in fresh water. Such instructions of course are rarely useful today, but they do serve to remind us about how much refrigeration has changed our diet and everyday life.

The sometimes surprisingly short cooking times for fresh meat in Mrs. Child's book provide another illustration of how cookery has changed. The times are short because the animals used for meat were not "improved," or specially bred for their meaty qualities, as they are for commercial use today. When Child's directions for roasting a lamb assume that the entire leg could cook in less than an hour, they refer to a young and comparatively skinny lamb bred for raising both wool and meat—not a much larger modern animal.

Because of comparable changes in how poultry is bred, the tradition of serving chicken pie along with the

Thanksgiving turkey has disappeared. In early New England, a turkey rarely weighed more than eight pounds, not enough to feed a large and hungry Thanksgiving crowd. Chicken pies once were used to extend the feast. Now that a cook can easily serve a twenty-five-pounder, they are not needed.

More than anything else, perhaps, it is the old way of writing recipes that makes them strange to us today. In some respects, they seem written in a foreign language. To begin with, there were few standardized measurements, and often no measurements at all. The cook was told to stop adding flour to Election Cake when the dough was "soft as it can be and still moulded on a board" or to cease adding cornmeal to hasty pudding "when it is so thick that you stir it with great difficulty." When Mrs. Child was specific about quantities, she called for flour by the pound, the quart or the cup, or sometimes by the teacupful—about three-quarters of a cup. For "Indian cake" (corn bread) she specified "a handful" of flour. She measured liquids in quarts, pints, and gills—a half-cup measure. In Mrs. Child's kitchen there was no set of standard measuring spoons. She referred at times to tablespoons and teaspoons, which sound familiar enough, but also measured ingredients with a "dessert spoon" (two-thirds of a tablespoon). She particularly favored using a "great spoon" while cooking—but its precise size is uncertain.

The leavening agents frequently used for cakes and quick breads included not only beaten eggs and yeast, but a trio of items not seen in today's kitchen—pearlash, saleratus, and "lively emptings." Pearlash, as its name suggests, was a gray powder derived from wood ashes. It worked much like baking powder. Saleratus was a bicarbonate of potash, like pearlash, but it contained more carbon dioxide. Baking soda is a good modern substitute for saleratus. "Lively emptings" were a handy substitute for eggs at a time when beer was commonly made at home. The "emptings" were the yeasty settlings of the beer barrel—what was left when the barrel was "emptied." In making doughnuts, for example, Mrs. Child recommended that a gill of lively emptings be mixed in with the flour and sugar instead of eggs.

Used in many thousands of American kitchens for many years, Mrs. Child's cookbook reflects the diet, foodways, and cooking practices of the early American republic better than any other. In 1843 the editor of *The Farmer's Monthly Visitor* recommended her book, now in its thirtieth edition, to the brides of New Hampshire: "It is adapted," he wrote, "to our country and the habits of our people. . . . Almost, if not quite all other works upon this subject are extravagant and not suited to the plain frugal wife." He went on to write that "Mrs. Child in her Frugal Housewife has won unfading laurels in producing that which is calculated to benefit the greatest number."[22] As a cookbook writer, Lydia Maria Child could have asked for no greater praise.

Notes

1. Mary A. Livermore, *The Story of My Life* (Hartford, Conn., 1899), pp. 404–6.
2. Samuel G. Goodrich, *A Pictorial Geography of the World* (Boston, 1840), p. 144.
3. Priscilla Robertson, *Lewis Farm: A New England Saga* (Norwood, Mass., c. 1952), pp. 140–41.
4. Dummerston, Vermont, Deeds, vol. 8, Clark Rice to Elijah Rice, Jan. 23, 1823.
5. Goodrich, *Pictorial Geography,* p. 144.
6. Susan I. Lesley, *Recollections of My Mother* (Boston, 1899), p. 417.
7. Sarah J. Hale, *The Way to Live Well and Be Well While We Live* (Philadelphia, 1839), p. 41.
8. Goodrich, *Pictorial Geography,* p. 144.
9. Lesley, *Recollections,* p. 419.
10. "The Adamses at Home, 1788–1886," *Proceedings of the Colonial Society of Massachusetts,* vol. 45 (1970), p. 15.
11. Edward E. Hale, *A New England Boyhood* (Boston, 1900), p. 115.
12. Mary E. Dewey, ed., *The Life and Letters of Catharine M. Sedgwick,* (New York, 1872), p. 102.
13. Lesley, *Recollections,* p. 421.
14. Journal of Ruth Henshaw Bascom, September 24, 1840, American Antiquarian Society, Worcester, Mass., in *The New-England Galaxy,* vol. 20, no. 3 (Winter 1979), p. 51.
15. Hale, *Boyhood,* p. 95.
16. "A Newburyport Wedding One Hundred and Thirty Years Ago," *Essex Institute Historical Collections,* vol. 87, no. 4, (October 1951), p. 313.
17. Alice J. Jones, *In Dover on the Charles* (Newport, R.I., 1906), p. 50.
18. Robert Roberts, *The House Servant's Directory* (Boston, 1827), reprint ed., Waltham, Mass., 1977, p. 63.
19. "The Adamses at Home," p. 47.
20. Lucy Larcom, *A New England Girlhood* (Boston, 1889), p. 98.
21. "Washington Cake," *The Farmer's Monthly Visitor* (April 29, 1843), p. 63.
22. "Instruction to Young Women," *The Farmer's Monthly Visitor* (August 31, 1843), p. 119.

Hearth Cookery

Most of us today have not learned hearth cookery at our mother's knee. Nor have cookbook authors of the past made it easy to reconstruct the methods used to prepare the recipes in their books. Lydia Maria Child, like the others, did not describe cooking techniques at length; rather, she assured her readers that there was no substitute for experience. Occasionally she mentions the cooking vessel to be used, but it is very difficult to match up her terminology with objects in museum collections of cooking equipment.

To cook with any degree of convenience at the hearth, it should be equipped with at least a pair of **andirons** and a swinging **crane**. If you must make a choice of cooking pots, a **Dutch oven** or **bake-kettle** offers the most flexibility for cooking over the fire and using coals on the hearth. In order to use the brick oven, a **metal shovel** for removing ashes is essential, and it can also be used for removing cooked food. However, a **peel**, a flat wooden shovel with a long handle, is the correct implement for taking cooked food from the oven. If you have only a flat metal shovel, it should be carefully cleaned after use to remove ashes.

Andirons are essential for building a fire, for they provide a base on which to build and provide for the circulation of air into the fire. It is possible to substitute a pair of quarter-split logs for andirons, but they will eventually become part of the fire. Metal andirons will last virtually forever. Early-nineteenth-century probate inventories of even the poorest dwellings include at least one pair of andirons, indicating that they were very common.

In order to hang pots over the fire to boil water, or for more extensive cooking projects, the hearth must be equipped with a mechanism for hanging a pot or kettle. A **crane**, built into the side of the fireplace, provides the most flexible way to suspend the pots, for the cook can swing it over the flames for cooking, and toward the hearth when adding ingredients to the pots or stirring and tasting the contents. To vary the height of the pot, an adjustable hook called a **trammel**, or one or more S-shaped iron hooks, may be used.

The first **cast-iron cooking pots**, made in Coalbrookdale, England, in the early eighteenth century, were revolutionary because they were the first durable vessels that could be heated directly and safely over a fire. They made cooking on the hearth far easier. In use for nearly 300 years, cast iron continues to have cooks who prefer it despite generations of innovation. By the early nineteenth century, a variety of cast-iron forms were being used for hearth cooking, in addition to the original **three-legged pot** which itself was made in many different sizes. The **hanging griddle** and **hanging skillet** were used for frying foods. Both are round with a semicircular handle for suspending the pan over the heat.

Another large pot, the **Dutch oven**, is deeper than the skillet but not as deep as the cooking pot. It has three legs, a handle, and a close-fitting lid. Early cookbooks are not specific about the how this piece of equipment was to be used. A **kettle** or **stew-kettle** is specified in some recipes in the "Common Cooking" section, for making chicken stews, in particular. One advantage of the Dutch oven is that it has a lid to cover a stew as it simmers. As its other name, "**bake-kettle**," suggests, it can also be heated and used to bake pies, biscuits, and puddings in place of the brick oven. To use it for baking, the pot and lid should be preheated in front of the fire. When the food is ready to be cooked, it should be placed inside the Dutch oven, which is then covered with the heated lid. It is placed over a bed of glowing coals drawn out from the fire, and more coals are shoveled on top of the lid. If the coals are not hot enough to cook the contents during the average baking time given in the recipe, fresh hot coals can be added so that cooking will continue.

A **spider** is another piece of cast-iron cooking equipment for use on the hearth. It is like a frying pan with legs that stands over a bed of coals. A **gridiron** is used for broiling meat; its open iron bars that support the meat gave its name to the markings on a football field. It also has feet and a long handle to simplify its use. A **wafer iron** is heated in the fire and removed for cooking. Place it on pads on a table, grease it, drop in a small quantity of batter, and then close it to cook. Three or

Spider

four wafers can normally be made before it needs to be heated again.

Cast-iron cooking utensils have a tendency to rust unless they are seasoned carefully before use and kept dry when not in use. To season a new utensil, rub corn or vegetable oil well across the entire interior and exterior of the pot before heating it over the fire. The oil will penetrate the iron to keep it from rusting. If it is used frequently to cook a variety of greasy and greaseless foods and dried thoroughly after each use, no rust spots will appear. If rust spots do appear with use, they should be thoroughly scoured with any commercial scouring pad to remove the rust before reseasoning the pot. A cast-iron pot should never be left standing with wet contents.

Iron trivets are indispensable in hearth cooking. They do not come into direct contact with the food; placed over coals, they are used to keep food warm or melt butter. Trivets are made in a variety of ornamental shapes and sizes, and it is useful to have more than one.

Traditionally, meat was roasted before the fire by inserting skewers through it and suspending it with a string from nails in the mantelpiece. But Mrs. Child recommends a **tin-kitchen**, sometimes called a **reflector oven**, as a far superior method of roasting.

A tin-kitchen is an elaborate half-cylinder shaped device built to stand before a hot fire, taking advantage of the heat and providing a curved base designed to catch drippings to be used for basting and making gravy. The meat is skewered to an iron spit and then inserted into the tin kitchen. The open side of the tin cylinder faces the flame.

The spit is rotated through a circular series of holes during the course of cooking. A small door allows the roast to be checked, "satisfying the curiosity of the cook." The instructions for making the gravy while the meat cooks, as given by Mrs. Child, direct that the meat be dredged with flour before it is placed in the oven. Boiling water poured into the well is used to baste the meat during cooking. After the meat is done, the gravy is poured off through a spout on the side and finished to the cook's taste before serving. After use, tin kitchens must be scoured and kept gleaming to preserve their reflecting quality.

Other tin utensils in nineteenth-century kitchens included tea and coffee pots and pie plates. In general, for baking in the brick oven or in a Dutch oven, **earthenware** (pottery) pie plates, bowls, and baking cups are preferable to tin, for they will withstand and evenly spread the heat of the oven without burning the food to be cooked. New England cooks used local redware pottery, which is still available from Old Sturbridge Village and other sources.

The Fire in the Hearth

Before any brick oven or fireplace is used, it should be checked thoroughly by a chimney sweep or other professional, and depending upon the amount of use, each type of chimney should be cleaned regularly. The brick oven must have a close-fitting door with a handle. For safety, it is recommended that a working fire extinguisher and an approved fire blanket be readily accessible. Baking soda for extinguishing a grease fire and a plentiful supply of water are also sensible safety precautions.

When selecting wood for a hearth fire, hardwood, if available, is best. It burns cleanly and produces less smoke. If the wood is damp, it will dry if it is kept indoors for a few days before it is used. If dry wood is needed in a hurry, place pieces of wood on end around the walls of the fireplace so that, as the fire burns, the wood will heat up and dry out for use.

Wood for cooking must be split. Pieces split into quarters will burn rapidly, providing the flames necessary for roasting and producing coals quickly for baking or cooking on the hearth. Small pieces split in half will burn more slowly with less flame. Kindling is needed for starting and maintaining the hearth fire and for heating the brick oven.

To build a fire on andirons, shovel old ashes and coals under them, leaving a 1-inch space to allow air to circulate. Use wood shavings if available, or roll pieces of dry newspaper into tight rolls or knots and place them on top of the ashes. Lay three or four pieces of kindling on the andirons, and place three or more pieces across these. Lay two pieces of wood split in quarters across the kindling, leaving an air space between them. Light the paper, starting at the back and working toward the front. Once the kindling has caught and is burning well, place two more pieces of quarter-split wood across the two already in place.

If you do not build the fire on andirons, lay two halves of a split log directly on the fireplace floor, perpendicular to the opening of the hearth. Using the logs as andirons, prepare the fire as directed above, leaving air spaces between the logs and the back wall of the fireplace.

After the basic fire has been built and is burning well, the fire may be adjusted according to the recipe that will be prepared. For a roaring fire needed for rapid cooking for reflector ovens, and to produce coals for use with Dutch ovens, use quarter-split dry wood. Stack the logs 3 inches apart to allow enough air to circulate for a clear-burning fire. Crisscross the logs with kindling. A roaring fire will produce coals quickly, usually within one or two hours.

A moderate fire is needed for boiling and stewing. Use a combination of quarter- and half-split dry wood, stacking them alternately for even heat.

A slow fire is needed for slow-cooking and soup stocks. Set half-split logs across the fire parallel to the opening of the fireplace, 1 to 2 inches apart. A slow fire will build up coals gradually after two to three hours.

From experience, we know that there are four common problems with hearth fires. But there are also solutions to each problem so that you as the cook can proceed with the recipe selected.

- A fire will not ignite properly if there is too little air. This happens when too much wood has been laid on it at the start, so that air does not circulate. When the fire is built, leave air spaces between the wood and kindling, especially when the wood is damp and will ignite only with dif-

ficulty. If the fire will not start, the only solution is to take it completely apart and rebuild it. Leave more air space and use less wood at first. Add more as the fire burns.

- If the top layer will not burn, more kindling may need to be added between layers. The kindling will flame and heat the top layer so that it will ignite.

- If the fire dies down too rapidly, the logs may be too close together. Use tongs to move the logs apart and create more air spaces. This problem may also be the result of using wood that is damp or too large. If so, more kindling may be needed underneath the logs.

- After you have removed the coals to use with a Dutch oven, the fire may die down rapidly, especially if it is burning in the slow-to-moderate range. This is because the coals provide a bed of heat that will keep the logs burning. To replace the coals, place dry kindling under the logs, so that they will burn more rapidly and form new coals.

When cooking is in progress, the heat can be controlled by the placement of the cookware and manipulation of the fire itself. When pots are hanging from a crane, they may be raised or lowered by using additional or fewer S-hooks or trammels. If quick heat or flames are required, small pieces of split, dry wood may be added to the fire. Kettles may be moved toward the end or the center of the crane, to be closer to or farther from the heat. Kettles on trammels may be moved away from or closer to the fire.

For slow-cooking, use a trivet over coals drawn out onto the hearth. For frying, melting butter, simmering, and making soft custards, the heat can be regulated by the frequency with which the coals are changed. Place a shovelful of coals on the hearth, and if your pots or skillets do not have legs, stand a wrought-iron trivet over the coals. For cooking quickly, change the coals often; for melting butter or cooking custards, change the coals less frequently.

When cooking with a reflector oven, move it closer to the fire if the meat is not browning rapidly, or farther away from the flame if the meat is burning in spots.

When Mrs. Child wrote her book, she had one kind of oven in mind. Today we would call it a **brick oven** or **bake-oven,** or even a beehive oven. Such an oven was constructed as part of the hearth with a large opening at about waist height. To heat this oven for use, the fire has to share the space with the food to be baked. "Experience and observation," Mrs. Child wrote, were the key ingredients for successful baking. "There is a great difference in the construction of ovens, and when an oven is extremely cold, either on account of the weather, or want of use, it must be heated more." Just as they did in her time, bake-ovens today vary in size and construction. Like our predecessors, you will have to become familiar with the oven you use because "no precise rules

for heating them can be given. . . . It is easy to find out how many sticks of a given size are necessary for baking articles that require a strong heat and so for those which are baked with less."

The fire in the bake-oven is laid on its floor, starting with shavings or newspaper on which kindling is arranged. Take five pieces of kindling, set them around and over the paper, and light them. When the first pieces of kindling have caught, gather up a handful of kindling and feed the fire, adding another three or four pieces, and then two or three more as you see the flames receding. (Do not replace the door until the oven is loaded with food to be baked.) Kindling will burn hotter and heat the oven more quickly. After an hour, writes Mrs. Child, "stir the fire equally to all parts of the oven. This is necessary for an equal diffusion of the heat. Do it several times before the oven is cleared."

The oven must preheat for two hours when pies and bread are to be baked. "Let the coals remain until they are no longer red. They should not look dead, but like hot embers. When you take them out, leave in the back part a few to be put near the pans that require most heat such as beans, Indian pudding, or jars of fruit. Before putting in the things to be baked, throw in a little flour. If it browns instantly, the oven is too hot and should stand open three or four minutes. If it browns without burning in the course of half a minute, it would be safe to set in the articles immediately." Use a peel or a flat wooden implement called a shovel to remove the coals. "Some sweep the walls of the oven with a wet broom to collect ashes which might get into the food." It is not necessary to use a thermometer to test the temperature, although when learning to fire a brick oven, it may help to learn how to gauge heat. The flour test is sufficient, or put your bare arm into the oven. If you can count to ten without feeling burned, it's not too hot to use.

As a general rule, an oven will heat in two hours. Obviously, it is much easier to let a hot oven cool down than to rekindle a fire.

Now the oven is ready to use. If it is large enough to bake several items at once, the following sequence and arrangement of items may be a helpful guide.

When the oven is hot, slow-cooking foods like beans and Indian pudding should be placed near the back wall, as they will not be removed for several hours. Foods requiring high heat, including pies, bread, biscuits, and cookies, are put in to cook as soon as possible after the oven is heated. After ten minutes, biscuits and cookies are baked and may be removed. The heat is now moderate and ready for cakes to bake. Thirty minutes after the fire has been removed, cakes will be cooked. The oven heat is now low for slow-cooking foods like custards and custard-based puddings and pies.

For the foods to cook properly, the oven should not be overcrowded. Foods to be baked are usually put into the oven in the reverse of the order in which they will be removed. In other words, beans go in first, come out last. Cookies go in last and come out first. This eliminates moving food around in the oven. When the door is open, cooler air rushes in and, as a result, breads and cakes may fall.

The **cast-iron bake-kettle** or **Dutch oven** is an alternative to the brick oven, especially if only one item is to be baked. To use the bake-kettle, build a roaring fire, or obtain coals from a moderate fire that has been burning for two hours or more. Depending on the heat required, the kettle may be heated by standing it against one of the andirons. Preheat the lid by standing it against the other andiron. For hot oven temperatures, preheat kettle and lid for a half hour. For the equivalent of a moderately hot oven, preheat for twenty minutes, and for a moderate oven ten minutes is sufficient. For custards and custard-based foods, do not preheat the kettle. If bread is to be baked, the lid may not require preheating. If the bread should rise more than a few inches, it may burn if it is too close to the hot lid. For bake-kettle cooking, the coals must have a clear, red-orange glow. If coals smoke when they are removed from the fire, they are not hot enough.

To use the bake-kettle, shovel two or three piles of coal onto the hearth, selecting a spot that will not be in the way of your movements around the hearth and oven. Set the kettle over the coals and place the food inside the kettle. Use a thick pot holder or two, and be careful not to touch the hot sides of the kettle. Set the lid on the kettle, and place two or three shovelfuls of coals on the lid. For food that will bake for a long period of time, the coals may be insulated by placing a layer of ashes over the coals on the lid and around the coals below the bake-kettle.

For pies, biscuits, and gingerbread, which require a higher baking temperature, coals may be changed every fifteen or twenty minutes. They may have to be changed after a shorter interval in cold weather, as they will cool more rapidly. Coals may be left up to forty-five minutes without being changed, especially for custards and puddings which must bake slowly at a lower temperature.

Although these directions are based on our experience at Old Sturbridge Village, they cannot be completely specific. Fires, fireplaces, and ovens are all subject to variation and individual preferences, as much now as in the past. Knowing one's equipment and ingredients comes as the result of practice. According to Mrs. Child, "Three things must be exactly right in order to have good bread. The quantity of the yeast, the lightness or fermentation of the dough, and the heat of the oven. No precise rules can be given to ascertain these points. It requires observation, reflection and a quick, nice judgment, to decide when all are right."

Today's hearth cooks have the luxury of learning how to prepare a big breakfast for a hungry family without having to get up in the early morning in a cold house. After some practice, you will be able to rise to such an occasion. First, you will need to learn about your own fireplace and how to build and sustain a cooking fire. Once you are familiar with cooking with the cast-iron utensils as well, you will thoroughly enjoy the results. That will make up for the extra labor involved in lugging and caring for equipment that was previously unfamiliar.

It is still possible to obtain the equipment for hearth cooking without using up antique originals. The special equipment may be obtained from blacksmiths and tinsmiths who exhibit at craft fairs and who work independently. In addition, the Museum Gift Shop at Old Sturbridge Village is always a source of the tin, iron, and pottery utensils that have traditionally been used. The Village reproductions have been specially selected for their authenticity.

Tin kitchens or reflector ovens are available, along with such small tin utensils as apple parers. Hand-wrought trivets, toasters, cranes, and hooks are offered, many made as demonstrations by Village blacksmiths. Commercially made hanging iron pots and skillets are generally in stock at the Village. New England redware pottery in traditional forms is hand thrown, glazed, and fired as a museum demonstration. Bean pots, pie plates, mixing bowls, and pitchers are among the forms available at all times. (For details on prices and shipping charges, contact the Museum Gift Shop, Old Sturbridge Village, Sturbridge, MA 01566; (508) 347-3362.)

While it is charming to cook in historical costume, or even a long dress, it is more practical, at least while learning, to wear jeans and other completely washable clothes. Since you will be hovering close to the fire, you cannot avoid the smoke. In the past, a woman's day was organized so that the majority of the family's cooking was done in the morning along with preparations for the midday meal. The morning costume included a cap, because covering the hair kept it a little cleaner. Women frequently changed their clothes for the afternoon, the time for sewing and visiting.

There are many ways to enjoy hearth cooking and appreciate a taste of the past with family and friends. Cooking at least part of a meal at the hearth is entertaining for all involved once you have begun to master the techniques. Before you feel confident enough to cook an entire multi-course meal for company at the hearth, why not plan to make part of the meal at the fireplace—the hors d'oeuvres perhaps, or a soup or the dessert. Several of the recipes included may be made in bite-size versions to nibble along with a drink.

Roasted cheese, codfish cakes, small sausage patties, and potato balls lend themselves readily to serve as appetizers, although Lydia Maria Child might be shocked at this adaptive use of the recipes of old. You might plan a simple menu, including soup and homemade bread. Cooking the soup over the fire on a winter's day keeps cook and guests together while the preparations are completed. For dessert, you might choose to use the wafer iron. You and your guests can stretch after the main course while helping to bake the thin cookies, roll them into cylinders, and fill them with whipped cream. Once you get started, you will think of other ways to make hearth cooking sociable and fun. There are some menu suggestions from nineteenth-century sources on pages 12 and 13. And remember, you don't have to cook at the hearth to re-create these meals.

COMMON COOKING

Roast Veal

Breast, shoulder, loin, or rolled roast of veal

½ cup butter

½ cup flour

1 teaspoon salt

1 teaspoon crushed marjoram or summer savory

½ teaspoon pepper

"The shoulder of veal is the most economical for roasting or boiling. Two dinners may be made from it—the shoulder roasted and the knuckle cut off to be boiled. Six or seven pounds of veal will roast in an hour and a half."

—The American Frugal Housewife, 1832

Modern Method:

1. Preheat oven to 450°F.

2. Melt butter and brush over meat. Mix flour, salt, and spices. Dredge meat with seasoned flour.

3. Place prepared meat on a rack in a pan in the oven. Reduce heat immediately to 300°F. Cook 30 minutes per pound.

Hearth Method:

1. Prepare reflector oven.

2. Run spit of reflector oven through center of roast. Secure with skewers.

3. Follow Step 2 in the Modern Method recipe.

4. Place spit in reflector oven. Stand reflector oven 6–10 inches from fire.

5. Turn meat at 20-minute intervals.

6. Cook 30 minutes per pound.

Yield: 4 servings per pound

Veal Cutlets

"Fried veal is better for being dipped in white of egg, and rolled in nicely pounded crumbs of bread, before it is cooked. One egg is enough for a common dinner."

—The American Frugal Housewife, 1832

1½ pounds veal cutlets, thinly sliced

2 egg whites

¾ cup dried bread crumbs

¼ cup butter or bacon fat for frying

Modern Method:

1. Beat egg whites in one shallow bowl or pie plate, and spread bread crumbs in another bowl.
2. Dip each slice of meat in the egg white and then coat with bread crumbs.
3. Melt fat in skillet, arrange meat and fry 3–4 minutes, until browned. Turn and fry on other side.

Hearth Method:

1. Follow Steps 1 and 2 in the Modern Method recipe.
2. Follow Step 3 in the Modern Method recipe, using a hanging skillet over a moderate fire.

Yield: 4–5 servings depending on number and thickness of slices

Pot Roast or Alamode Beef

STUFFING:

2 cups grated bread crumbs

¼ cup finely chopped suet

1 teaspoon herbs: basil, thyme, sage, or parsley

½ teaspoon pepper

¼ teaspoon nutmeg

¼ teaspoon cloves

1 teaspoon salt

1 egg yolk

POT ROAST:

5 or more pounds beef: brisket, rump, chuck, shoulder

Cheesecloth to wrap meat, optional

String

2 cups boiling water, more for hearth cookery

2 cups claret

½ teaspoon allspice

½ teaspoon cloves

"Tie up a round of beef so as to keep it in shape; make a stuffing of grated bread, suet, sweet herbs, quarter of an ounce of nutmeg, a few cloves pounded, yolk of an egg. Cut holes in the beef, and put in stuffing, leaving about half the stuffing to be made into balls. Tie the beef up in a cloth, just to cover it with water, let it boil an hour and a half; then turn it, and let it boil an hour and a half more; then turn out the liquor, and put some skewers across the bottom of the pot, and lay the beef upon it, to brown; turn it that it may brown on both sides. Put a pint of claret, and some allspice and cloves, into the liquor, and boil some balls made of the stuffing in it."

—*The American Frugal Housewife*, 1832

Modern Method:

1. Combine bread crumbs, suet, herbs, salt, and egg yolk to make stuffing.
2. Cut holes into the roast to insert half of stuffing mixture. Make remaining stuffing mixture into 1-inch balls and chill.
3. Wrapping the meat is optional. (Cover meat with a clean white cheesecloth and tie securely with string.) Put meat into an ovenproof baking dish with a lid. Add boiling water. (Add additional ½ cup of water for every pound over 5 pounds.)
4. Bake in 300°F oven or simmer on top of stove for 2½–3 hours, turning meat several times while cooking.
5. Pour broth into a heavy saucepan, and simmer to reduce by half. Leave meat in baking dish and return to oven to brown while gravy is made.
6. Add claret and spices to broth. Bring almost to a boil before dropping in stuffing balls. Simmer 15 minutes before serving.

Hearth Method:

1. Follow Steps 1 and 2 in the Modern Method recipe.

2. Wrapping the meat is optional. (Cover meat with a clean white cheesecloth and tie securely with string.)

3. Place meat in preheated heavy hanging kettle with lid. Just cover with hot water and bring to a rapid boil over a hot fire.

4. Maintain boiling or close to boiling temperatures for 1½ hours. Then turn meat and check cooking liquid to see that it is not boiled away and boil for 1½ hours longer.

5. Take meat out of pot, remove cheesecloth, and brown on all sides in a hanging skillet or over hot coals.

6. While the meat is being browned, continue to cook the broth over hot fire until it is reduced by half. Add claret, allspice, and cloves. Drop stuffing balls into gravy. Simmer for 15 minutes before serving.

Yield: 2 servings per pound

Mince Meat, to Serve on Toast

2 cups leftover roast, pot roast, etc.

1 cup cooked chopped vegetables

Beef drippings or butter

2 cups apples, pared, cored, and sliced

2–3 cups gravy

½ teaspoon sage

Toast points

"There is a great difference in preparing mince meat. Some make it a coarse, unsavory dish; and others make it nice and palatable. No economical house-keeper will despise it; for broken bits of meat and vegetables cannot so well be disposed of in any other way. If you wish to have it nice, mash your vegetables fine, and chop your meat very fine. Warm it with what remains of sweet gravy or roast-meat drippings, you may happen to have. Two or three apples, pared, cored, sliced and fried, to mix with it, is an improvement. Some like a little sifted sage sprinkled in.

It is generally considered nicer to chop your meat fine, warm it in gravy, season it, and lay it upon a large slice of toasted bread to be brought upon the table without being mixed with potatoes but if you have cold vegetables, use them."

—*The American Frugal Housewife*, 1832

Modern Method:

1. Chop leftover roast. Combine meat and vegetables.
2. Melt drippings or butter in a large skillet and fry apples until soft.
3. Make a gravy by combining 1 cup each of flour and water, heated and seasoned with salt and pepper.
4. Add chopped meat, vegetables, gravy, and sage to the apples in the skillet and heat slowly.
5. Serve on toast.

Hearth Method:

1. Follow Steps 1–4 in the Modern Method recipe, using a large hanging skillet.

Yield: 6 servings

Beef Steak

"The quicker beef-steak can be broiled the better. Seasoned after it is taken from the grid-iron. The richest, tenderest and most delicate piece of beef for steak is the rump and the last cut of the sirloin."

—The American Frugal Housewife, 1832

Sirloin, T–bone, or porterhouse steak, 2 inches thick

Modern Method:

1. Preheat broiler.
2. Let steak warm to room temperature before broiling.
3. Broil 5–7 minutes on first side; turn and broil 4–5 minutes.

Hearth Method:

1. Preheat gridiron over coals.
2. Put steak on gridiron and put fresh coals below.
3. Broil for 5–7 minutes.
4. Turn meat and place gridiron over fresh coals.
5. Broil 5 minutes.

Yield: 2–3 servings per pound

Roast Beef

Rib, sirloin, or other beef suitable for oven roasting

"A quarter of an hour to each pound of beef is considered a good rule for roasting; but this is too much when the bone is large and the meat thin. Six pounds of the rump should roast six quarters of an hour, but bony pieces less. It should be done before a quick fire. The richest, tenderest and most delicate piece of beef for roasting is the rump and the last cut of the sirloin. If economy be consulted instead of luxury, the round will be bought in preference to the rump."

—The American Frugal Housewife, 1832.

Modern Method:

1. Preheat the oven to 500°F.
2. Place the roast, fat-side up, on a rack in a pan, and reduce heat to 350°F.
3. For medium to medium rare, cook 18–20 minutes per pound. If cooking a rolled roast, allow 25 minutes per pound.

Hearth Method:

1. Prepare reflector oven.
2. Run spit through meat lengthwise, and secure with skewers.
3. Place reflector oven 6–10 inches from fire.
4. Allow 20–25 minutes per pound, turning spit every 20 minutes.

Yield: 3–4 servings per pound if boneless cut of beef is used
1–2 servings per pound if meat has bone

Corned Beef

"When you merely want to corn meat, you have nothing to do but to rub in salt plentifully and let it set in the cellar a day or two. The navel end of the brisket is one of the best pieces for corning.

"A six pound piece of corned beef should boil three full hours. Put it in to boil when the water is cold. If you boil it in a small pot, it is well to change the water, when it has boiled an hour and a half; the fresh water should boil before the half-cooked meat is put in again."

—The American Frugal Housewife, 1832

2 cups salt

1 gallon hot water

3–6 pounds brisket of beef

Cold water to cover meat

Note: The term *corned* refers to the "corns" or grains of salt used to preserve the beef.

Modern Method:

1. To corn the beef, make up a brine solution by dissolving 1½ cups of salt in a gallon of hot water in a large enameled, glass, or stoneware pot. Cool.
2. Rub remaining ½ cup salt into meat. Place the meat in the cooled brine solution, covering with a weight to keep the meat submerged in the brine. Refrigerate or set in a cool place for 48 hours.
3. To cook, rinse meat and place in a large cooking pot with a lid. Cover with water and bring to a boil.
4. Simmer, covered, 3–4 hours, until tender. Add more boiling water, if necessary.

Hearth Method:

1. Follow Steps 1 and 2 in the Modern Method recipe.
2. Follow Step 3 in the Modern Method recipe, using a large hanging pot.
3. Simmer 3–4 hours, adding more boiling water if necessary. Make sure that the fire is hot enough for the water in the pot to simmer for the entire cooking period.

Yield: 2–3 servings per pound

Pork Sausage

1 pound salted casings (if link sausages are desired)

1 pound lean ground or finely chopped pork

3 teaspoons powdered sage

1½ teaspoons salt

1 teaspoon pepper

"Three teaspoons of powdered sage, one and a half of salt and one of pepper, to a pound of meat, is good seasoning for sausages."

—*The American Frugal Housewife*, 1832

Modern Method and Hearth Method:

1. Soak casings in cold water, according to package directions. Drain and place on towels to dry off, but keep moist for use.

2. Blend pork and seasonings thoroughly.

3. Stuff casings using a manual sausage stuffer or electric grinder attachment. If a manual stuffer is used, warm meat slightly before stuffing the casings. Or shape seasoned meat into patties.

4. Fry over low heat until well cooked in a skillet on a stove or over a hot fire at the hearth.

Yield: 4 servings

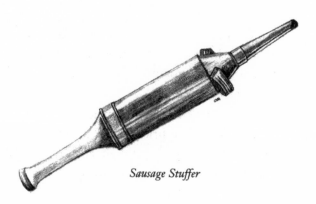

Sausage Stuffer

Pork Roast

"Fresh pork should be cooked more than any other meat. A thick shoulder piece should be roasted full two hours and a half; and other pieces less in proportion."

—*The American Frugal Housewife*, 1832

Loin rib or shoulder of pork

1 cup flour

1 teaspoon salt

1 teaspoon sage

½ teaspoon pepper

1 cup water

Modern Method:

1. Preheat oven to 450°F.
2. If gravy is desired, mix the flour, salt, sage, and pepper and dredge seasoned flour over meat and place on rack in a pan. Pour water into pan. Reduce oven heat immediately to 350°F.
3. Cook rolled or boneless roast 40 minutes per pound. Cook a loin or rib roast with bones in for 30–35 minutes per pound.

Hearth Method:

1. Prepare reflector oven.
2. Run spit through center of roast; secure with skewers. If gravy is desired, mix the flour, salt, sage, and pepper, and dredge seasoned flour over meat. Pour water into base of reflector oven, and set in front of fire 6–10 inches away from it.
3. Follow Step 3 in the Modern Method recipe, turning the spit at 20-minute intervals.

Yield: 2–3 servings per pound

Pork Apple Pie

1½ cups leftover roast pork, cut in thin slices

3 cups apples, cut in thin slices

1 cup brown sugar

1 teaspoon allspice

Piecrust for a two-crust pie (recipe on page 135)

"Make your crust in the usual manner, spread it over a large deep plate, cut some slices of fat pork very thin, also some slices of apple; place a layer of apples, and then of pork, with a very little allspice, and pepper, and sugar, between—three or four layers of each, with crust over the top. Bake one hour."

—*The New England Economical Housekeeper,* 1845

Modern Method:

1. Prepare the piecrust and place lower crust into pie plate.
2. Layer slices of apple and pork. Sprinkle with brown sugar and allspice.
3. Cover with top crust. Bake in preheated 400°F oven for 1 hour.

Hearth Method:

1. Follow Steps 1–3 in the Modern Method recipe.
2. Bake for 1 hour in a bake oven or bake-kettle that has been preheated 15 minutes. If using the bake-kettle, change coals after 25 minutes of baking.

Yield: one pie

Salt Pork and Apples

"Fried salt pork and apples is a favorite dish in the country, but it is seldom seen in the city. After the pork is fried, some of the fat should be taken out, lest the apples should be oily. Acid apples should be chosen, because they cook more easily; they should be cut in slices across the whole apple, about twice or three times as thick as a new dollar. Fried until tender and brown on both sides—laid around the pork. If you have cold potatoes, slice them and brown them in the same way."

—*The American Frugal Housewife*, 1832

1–2 thick slices salt pork

3 medium apples

2–3 cooked potatoes

1 pound pork, cut up, or 4–6 pork chops

Modern Method:

1. Cut salt pork into small thin pieces and render the fat.

2. Core and slice the apples, and slice the potatoes.

3. Cook cut-up pork or chops in the pan in which the salt pork has been rendered. Fry 20–25 minutes.

4. If skillet is large enough, push meat to one side; otherwise transfer to serving platter and keep warm. Check to see if there is sufficient fat for frying. If not, render a second slice of salt pork to fry apples and potatoes until browned.

5. To serve, arrange fried apples and potatoes around meat on serving platter.

Hearth Method:

1. Follow Steps 1 and 2 in the Modern Method recipe.

2. Render salt pork in a hanging skillet. Add cut-up pork or chops and fry 20–25 minutes.

3. Follow Steps 4 and 5 in the Modern Method recipe.

Yield: 4 servings

Beans

1 pound dried beans

Water to cover beans

¾ pound boneless pork, cubed

½ pound salt pork, cut in thin slices

1 teaspoon pepper

"Baked beans are a very simple dish, yet few cook them well. They should be put in cold water, and hung over the fire, the night before they are baked. In the morning, they should be put in a colander, and rinsed two or three times; then again placed in a kettle, with the pork you intend to bake, covered with water, and kept scalding hot, an hour or more. A pound of pork is quite enough for a quart of beans, and that is a large dinner for a common family. The rind of the pork should be slashed. Pieces of pork alternately fat and lean, are the most suitable; the cheeks are the best. A little pepper sprinkled among the beans, when they are placed in the bean-pot, will render them less unhealthy. They should be just covered with water, when put into the oven; and the pork should be sunk a little below the surface of the beans. Bake three or four hours."

—*The American Frugal Housewife*, 1832

Note: This recipe is intended to make an economical meal by stretching the pork with the addition of beans. Mrs. Child is describing "pieces of pork" that are both "fat and lean," rather than fatty chunks of salt pork as you would purchase in a supermarket today. This recipe does not call for any brown sugar or molasses but is flavored instead by the slices of pork and ground pepper. In her 1845 cookbook, Esther A. Howland recommended that the cook "dissolve a lump of saleratus as big as a walnut with your beans before making and you will find them greatly improved." *Saleratus* is baking soda.

Bean Pot

Modern Method:

1. Soak beans in water at room temperature overnight.

2. Drain, reserving water. Rinse beans thoroughly.

3. Layer beans and pork in a heavy saucepan. Add reserved water. Bring to boil and simmer for 1 hour.

4. To bake, transfer beans, pork, and water into a bean pot or other ovenproof casserole with a lid. Season with pepper. There should be enough liquid to just cover beans. Add hot water, if necessary.

5. Bake 4–6 hours. If a Crock-Pot or slow-cooker is used, cook beans and pork on high heat for an hour or more. Turn heat to low and cook 10–12 hours or overnight.

Hearth Method:

1. Soak beans in water overnight. If fireplace has been used, hang beans in a pot of water over remaining coals, otherwise soak in a bowl at room temperature.

2. Follow Step 2 in the Modern Method recipe.

3. Layer beans and pork in a hanging kettle. Add reserved water. Bring to a boil over a hot fire and cook for 1 hour.

4. To bake, transfer beans, pork, and water to a bean pot. Season with pepper.

5. Place bean pot toward the back of a preheated brick oven, where it will not be disturbed as other foods are baked. Leave 4–6 hours or overnight. As the oven cools, the beans will cook.

Yield: 8 cups or more depending on variety of beans used

Roast Lamb or Mutton

5 pounds leg or shoulder of lamb or mutton

1 teaspoon crushed sage or summer savory

"Six or seven pounds of mutton will roast in an hour and a half. Lamb one hour. The breast or shoulder of mutton are both nice for roasting, boiling or broth. The loin of lamb is suitable for roasting."

—The American Frugal Housewife, 1832

Modern Method:

1. Preheat oven to 450°F.
2. To prepare meat for cooking remove the fell, the paper-like outside covering. Using a pointed knife, insert pinches of crushed herbs under the skin.
3. Place meat, fat-side up, on a pan with a rack and put in the oven. Reduce the heat immediately to 350°F and roast 25 minutes per pound.

Hearth Method:

1. Prepare reflector oven.
2. Follow Steps 2 and 3 in the Modern Method recipe.
3. Insert spit of reflector oven through meat and secure with skewers. Put reflector oven in front of the fire.
4. Cook 25 minutes to the pound, rotating spit every 20 minutes.

Yield: 6–7 servings

"At one o'clock came dinner; always a large joint roast or boiled, with plenty of vegetables and few condiments,—for she thought them unwholesome, good bread and butter and a plain pudding or pie.

"If it was to be a tea-party, she had only to order an abundant supply of tea and coffee, with thin slices of bread and butter doubled, sponge cake made by the daughters before breakfast and thin slices of cold tongue or ham; if an evening party, the lemonade and cake and wine in summer, and the nuts and raisins and fine apples in winter, furnished the simple but sufficient entertainment."

—Susan I. Lesley, *Recollections of My Mother* (Boston, 1899)

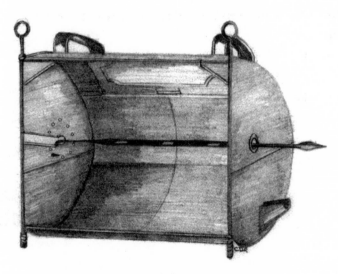

Tin Kitchen

Turkey

1 turkey, approximately 8
pounds

STUFFING:
6 common crackers or ½ loaf
of bread

½ cup finely chopped salt
pork

1 teaspoon sage

½ teaspoon summer savory
or sweet marjoram, optional

½ teaspoon pepper

1 egg

GRAVY (FOR HEARTH
METHOD):
1 cup water

1 cup flour

Salt and pepper to taste

"A good sized turkey [about 8 pounds back then—Ed.] *should be roasted two hours and a half, or three hours; very slowly at first. If you wish to make plain stuffing, pound a cracker, or crumble some bread very fine, chop some raw salt pork very fine, sift some sage, (and summer savory, or sweet marjoram, if you have them in the house, and fancy them,) and mould them all together, seasoned with a little pepper. An egg worked in makes the stuffing cut better; but it is not worth while when eggs are dear. About the same length of time is required for boiling and roasting."*

—The American Frugal Housewife, 1832

Modern Method:

1. Preheat oven to 450°F.
2. Pound crackers or grate bread into soft crumbs.
3. Mix remaining ingredients with cracker or bread crumbs.
4. Stuff the bird and secure the cavity with poultry lacers or sew it together.
5. Put bird on a rack in a pan and into the oven. Reduce heat to 350°F. Roast 25 minutes per pound.

Hearth Method:

1. Prepare fire and reflector oven.
2. Follow Steps 2–4 in the Modern Method recipe.
3. Push spit through the bird parallel to the backbone. The number of skewers needed will depend on the size of the bird. Push skewers at a right angle to spit, securing them through the holes in the spit. Using string, tie legs and wings securely to the bird. Dredge bird with flour and salt mixture.

4. Insert spit in tin kitchen; place it 10–12 inches from the fire. Rotate spit every 15 minutes. Dredge with remainder of flour and pour hot water over bird after 1 hour and move oven toward fire, so that it is 6–8 inches away from heat. Roast about 25 minutes per pound. When bird is done, remove from spit to serve.

5. If gravy is desired, skim off extra fat and add flour 1 tablespoon at a time. Heat to boiling to cook the flour thoroughly before serving. Salt and pepper to taste.

Yield: 1 serving per pound

Broiled Chicken

Broiling chicken 2–3 pounds, cut up

1 cup water

¼ cup butter, optional

"In broiling chickens, it is difficult to do the inside of the thickest pieces without scorching the outside. It is a good plan to parboil them about 10 minutes in a spider or skillet, covered close to keep the steam in, then put them upon the gridiron, broil and butter. It is a good plan to cover them with a plate, while on the gridiron. They may be basted with a very little of the water in which they were parboiled; and if you have company who like melted butter to pour upon the chicken, the remainder of the liquor will be good used for that purpose."

—The American Frugal Housewife, 1832

Modern Method:

1. Preheat broiler or barbecue grill.
2. Parboil chicken in water in a tightly covered pan for 10 minutes.
3. Put chicken, skin-side down, on preheated broiling pan. Reserve broth.
4. Broil 10 minutes, turn and baste with reserved broth. Broil 8–10 minutes more, or until browned.
5. Serve with melted butter, if desired.

Hearth Method:

1. Follow Step 2 in the Modern Method recipe.
2. Draw coals out onto hearth, and preheat gridiron. Arrange chicken parts and cover with a plate. Reserve broth. Broil 25 minutes.
3. Turn chicken, draw out more coals, put gridiron over fresh coals, and baste with reserved broth. Cover and broil 20 minutes.
4. Melt butter or heat remaining broth in front of fire.
5. Place chicken on a warmed serving platter. Pass melted butter or broth, if desired.

Yield: 1 serving per ¾ pound

Stewed Chicken, *with Broth to Serve Separately*

"Chickens should boil about an hour. If old, they should boil longer. In as little water as will cook them. Chicken broth made like mutton broth.

"If your family like broth, throw in some clear rice when you put in the meat. The rice should be in proportion to the quantity of broth you mean to make. A large tablespoonful is enough for three pints of water. Seasoned with a very little pepper and salt. Summer savory, or sage, rubbed through a sieve, thrown in."

—*The American Frugal Housewife*, 1832

4- or 5-pound whole chicken, washed

2 cups water, more for hearth cookery

2–4 tablespoons rice

1 teaspoon salt

½ teaspoon pepper

1 teaspoon sifted summer savory or sage

Modern Method:

1. Place chicken in a saucepan with 2 cups water. Add rice and seasonings if flavored broth or chicken soup is desired.

2. Bring to a boil, skim the pot, cover and simmer for 1¼ hours.

3. When cooked, remove chicken from broth. The chicken may be served hot or cooled for use in chicken salad (see note). Chicken broth with rice should be refrigerated until ready to use.

Hearth Method:

1. Place whole chicken in a hanging kettle. Add cold water until chicken is almost covered. Add rice and seasonings if broth or soup is desired.

2. Bring to a boil over hot fire, pull away from heat to skim. Cover pot and simmer for 1½ hours.

3. Follow Step 3 in recipe above.

Yield: 5–6 servings

Note: A serving suggestion from the nineteenth century is to cut a small head of cabbage into wedges and add to pot for the last ½ hour of cooking. In the past, this was a frequent combination, served even at Thanksgiving.

Roast Chicken with Stuffing

STUFFING:
4–5 slices of bread: flour, rye, whole wheat, corn, etc.

4 tablespoons butter

Salt and pepper to taste

4- or 5-pound roasting chicken

GRAVY:
1 cup water

1 cup flour

Salt and pepper to taste

"An hour is enough for common sized chickens to roast. A smart fire is better than a slow one; but they must be tended closely. Slices of bread, buttered, salted and peppered, put into the stomach (not the crop) are excellent."

—*The American Frugal Housewife,* 1832

Modern Method:

1. Preheat oven to 450°F.
2. Slice bread, and butter and season to taste. Fill cavity loosely and secure the opening with poultry lacers for a large bird, or by sewing it closed for a smaller one.
3. For gravy, sift flour, salt, and pepper together and dredge half of mixture over poultry.
4. Place on rack in a pan. Reduce heat to 350°F. Roast 20 minutes per pound.
5. After 1 hour, shake remaining flour, salt, and pepper over bird and pour 1 cup boiling water over it.
6. When chicken is cooked, finish gravy by skimming off extra fat or adding flour, if needed. Cook to blend, correct seasoning, and serve hot.

Hearth Method:

1. Prepare reflector oven.
2. Slice bread, and butter and season to taste. Fill cavity loosely, reserving the crust of bread for last to cover opening of cavity.
3. For gravy, place water in base of reflector oven and dredge the bird with half of the seasoned flour.
4. Run spit through prepared bird, securing legs and wings with string.
5. Insert spit in reflector oven and place 6–10 inches from fire. Rotate spit every 20 minutes.

6. For gravy, halfway through cooking period, dredge remaining seasoned flour over bird and baste with hot water.

7. When chicken is cooked, remove from spit. Ladle or pour gravy mixture into a hanging skillet. Remove fat or add flour, as required. Cook to blend, correct seasoning, and serve hot.

Yield: 1 serving per ¾ pound

Roasting Chicken on a String

"In the absence of spits, a good stout nail with a strong string or skein of worsted, will dangle a joint and if the fire be made proportionably high to the length of the joint, there is no better mode of roasting. A strong skewer must be run in at each end of the joint, in order that it may be turned."

—The American Frugal Housewife, 1832

Natural-fiber string (candle wicking and garden string work well, as do cotton shoelaces)

Two iron skewers

Roasting chicken

Stuffing, optional (recipe on page 48)

Hearth Method:

1. The hearth must have a nail driven into the brick facing or the mantelpiece, from which the chicken will be suspended before the fire.

2. Cut two pieces of strong string, one about 18 inches, the other long enough to reach from the nail to a point 24 inches above the floor. Tie a loop on each end of both lengths of string, large enough to slip off the skewers easily. Run the shorter string through the loop on the bottom of the longer string, forming a T. This will be the lower end of the string.

3. If the chicken is to be stuffed, do so now, filling the cavity loosely.

4. Insert one iron skewer through the chicken, catching the wings. Insert the other skewer through the chicken legs below the bone, thus securing the legs and catching the flap of skin to hold in the stuffing.

5. Hook the two loops of the shorter string to the ends of the skewer that goes through the legs so that the chicken is upright and will retain the juices in the initial cooking period. Hook the loop at the top end of the longer string over the nail. Place a bowl or spider below the suspended chicken to catch the drippings.

6. Twist the suspended string as often as you can to start the turning motion, giving it a twist each time you go past. The longer the string, the more evenly the bird will cook because it will be turning more of the time.

7. Calculate the cooking time for a stuffed chicken at 25 minutes per pound, but be prepared to add time at the end if the fire is not kept sufficiently hot and the

chicken juices are not running clear. Keep the fire burning briskly throughout cooking time. Halfway through, the chicken will need to be re-hung. Place a plate under the meat, slip the string from each side of the top skewer, and reattach the loops to the bottom skewer, which now becomes the top skewer. Re-twist string and continue cooking. When the chicken is browned, use the drippings as a base for gravy, if desired.

Yield: one roast chicken

Chicken on a String

Chicken Fricassee, Brown

3–4 pounds chicken, cut up, or parts

2–3 onions

¾ cup flour

1 teaspoon salt

1 teaspoon pepper

¼–½ cup butter

2 cups boiling water

1 tablespoon sage or marjoram

½ lemon, optional

½ cup catsup, optional (recipe on page 200)

"Singe the chickens; cut them in pieces; pepper, salt, and flour them; fry them in fresh butter, till they are very brown: take the chickens out, and make a good gravy, into which put sweet herbs (marjoram or sage) according to your taste; if necessary, add pepper and salt; butter and flour must be used in making the gravy, in such quantities as to suit yourself for thickness and richness. After this is all prepared, the chicken must be stewed in it, for half an hour, closely covered. A pint of gravy is about enough for two chickens; I should think a piece of butter about as big as a walnut, and a table-spoonful of flour, would be enough for the gravy. The herbs should, of course, be pounded and sifted. Some, who love onions, slice two or three, and brown them with the chicken. Some slice a half lemon, and stew with the chicken. Some add tomatoes catsup."

—The American Frugal Housewife, 1832

Note: Fricassee is formed from the French words *frire* (to fry) and *casser* (to break), which describe the cooking technique employed in this dish. The chicken is cut into pieces and then fried. Fricassee also utilizes another often-used method of preparing chicken—twice-cooking. The chicken is first fried and then simmered or stewed, which tenderizes the fowl.

Modern Method:
1. Slice onions and lemon, and set aside.
2. Rinse chicken.
3. Mix flour, salt, and pepper. Dredge chicken with seasoned flour. Reserve leftover seasoned flour.
4. Melt butter in a large skillet or flame-proof casserole with a cover. Fry chicken pieces for 5 minutes on each side, or until browned. Add more butter, if needed. Remove chicken. Fry onions and push aside.
5. There should be about 2 tablespoons or more of butter left in the skillet. Add an equal amount of the remaining seasoned flour. Stir to make a paste, cook briefly,

and then add boiling water, stirring until gravy thickens.

6. Season with herbs and lemon or catsup, if desired. Add chicken. Cover closely and simmer for about ½ hour. If there is too much fat, skim it off before serving.

Hearth Method:

1. Follow Steps 1–3 in the Modern Method recipe.

2. Melt butter in a hanging pot or large hanging skillet. Fry chicken pieces for five minutes on each side or until browned. Add more butter, if needed. Remove chicken. Fry onions.

3. Push onions to one side and allow remaining butter to drain down to one edge of skillet. There should be 2 tablespoons or more butter remaining in skillet. Add an equal amount of the remaining seasoned flour. Stir to make a paste, push pot back over fire, and cook briefly. Carefully add boiling water away from the fire, stirring until gravy thickens.

4. Follow Step 6 in the Modern Method recipe.

Yield: 1 serving per ¾ pound

Chicken Fricassee, White

3-pound whole chicken, or parts

Large onion, optional

2 tablespoons butter

2 tablespoons flour

1½ cups hot water or broth

1 teaspoon salt

½ teaspoon pepper

½ teaspoon mace

1 tablespoon sage or marjoram

2 egg yolks

¼ cup cream

¼ teaspoon nutmeg

Juice of ½ lemon

"The chickens are cut to pieces, and covered with warm water, to draw out the blood. Then put into a stew-pan, with three quarters of a pint of water, or veal broth, salt, pepper, flour, butter, mace, sweet herbs pounded and sifted; boil it half an hour. If it is too fat, skim it a little. Just before it is done, mix the yolk of two eggs with a gill of cream, grate in a little nutmeg, stir it up till it is thick and smooth, squeeze in half a lemon. If you like onions, stew some slices with the other ingredients."

—The American Frugal Housewife, 1832

Modern Method:

1. Cut chicken into small pieces (soak in warm water only if freshly killed). If desired, cut onion into thin slices.
2. In a large skillet or flame-proof casserole, melt butter and add flour to make a paste. Stir in hot water or broth, and continue stirring until it thickens. Add chicken, onion if desired, salt, pepper, mace, and sage or marjoram. Cook for 30–45 minutes in all. Before serving, skim fat if necessary.
3. Just before serving, beat egg yolks, and add cream and nutmeg. Pour slowly into chicken and sauce. Squeeze lemon over all and heat through, but do not boil.

Hearth Method:

1. Follow Steps 1 and 2 in the Modern Method recipe, using a hanging skillet.
2. Follow Step 3 in the Modern Method recipe, removing skillet from fire to add ingredients.

Yield: 1 serving per ¾ pound

Curried Fowl

"Fry out two or three slices of salt pork; cut the chicken in pieces, and lay it in the stew-pan with one sliced onion; when the fowl is tender, take it out, and put in thickening into the liquor, one spoonful of flour, and one spoonful of curry-powder, well stirred up in water. Then lay the chicken in again, and let it boil up a few minutes. A half a pint of liquor is enough for one chicken. About half an hour's stewing is necessary. The juice of half a lemon improves it; and some like a spoonful of tomatoes catsup."

—*The American Frugal Housewife,* 1832

3-pound chicken, or parts

1 medium onion

3 slices salt pork, ¼-inch thick

2 cups water, more for hearth cookery

2 tablespoons flour

2 tablespoons curry powder

½ cup water

Juice of ½ lemon, optional

1 tablespoon catsup, optional (recipe on page 200)

Modern Method:

1. Wash chicken and cut into pieces; slice the onion and chop the pork.
2. Fry salt pork in a deep skillet or flame-proof casserole until crisp. Remove crisped pork.
3. Sauté onion in hot fat and push aside. Brown chicken on both sides.
4. Cover with water and simmer ½ hour until chicken is tender. Remove chicken.
5. Mix flour, curry powder, and water. Stir into cooking juices and cook 5 minutes or until thickened. Add lemon and/or catsup, if desired.
6. Put the chicken back into the skillet and reheat before serving.

Hearth Method:

1. Follow Step 1 in the Modern Method recipe.
2. In a hanging skillet, fry salt pork until crisp. Pull from direct heat and remove crisped pork.
3. Follow Step 3 in the Modern Method recipe.
4. Add 2 cups water, or a little more to cover the chicken. Bring to a boil and simmer for ½ hour until chicken is tender. Pull off heat and remove chicken.
5. Mix flour, curry powder, and water. Stir into cooking juices and return to fire. Cook 5 minutes or until thickened. Add lemon and/or catsup, if desired.
6. Follow Step 6 in Modern Method recipe.

Yield: 1 serving per ¾ pound

"May Fortune be always an attendant on Virtue."

"May mirth and good fellowship be always in fashion."

"Success to the fair sex in all their undertakings."

"May help bind him whom honor can't."

"May we never taste the Apples of Affliction."

—*Arithmetic Schoolbook,* manuscript circa 1792, Old Sturbridge Village Research Library

Ham

"Early in the morning put it into a large pot or kettle with plenty of cold water. Place it over a slow fire that it may heat gradually; it should not come to a boil in less than an hour and a half, or two hours. When it boils, quicken the fire, and skim the pot carefully. Then simmer it gently four or five hours or more, according to its size. A ham weighing fifteen pounds should simmer five hours after it has come to a boil."

—Directions for Cookery, 1851

1 smoked ham

Water to cover ham

Modern Method:

1. Select a pot large enough to hold ham and plenty of cold water.
2. Bring to a boil, reduce heat and simmer uncovered 20–30 minutes per pound.

Hearth Method:

1. Use a large hanging pot. Cover ham with cold water and place over a hot fire until it comes to a simmer.
2. Maintain simmer, allowing 20–30 minutes per pound.

Yield: 2–3 servings per pound

Meat Pie

PIECRUST FOR 9-INCH PIE:
2 cups flour

⅓ cup lard or other shortening

¼ cup water

FILLING:
2–3 cups cooked chicken, giblets, parboiled cut-up whole chicken, or any other cooked, chopped meat

¼ cup chopped salt pork

2 eggs

1 cup meat gravy or 1 cup chicken broth and ¼ cup flour

Salt and pepper to taste

"A nice way of serving up cold chicken, or pieces of cold fresh meat, is to make them into a meat pie. The gizzards, livers, and necks of poultry, parboiled, are good for the same purpose. If you wish to bake your meat pie, line a deep earthen or tin pan with paste made of flour, cold water, and lard; use but little lard, for the fat of the meat will shorten the crust. Lay in your bits of meat, or chicken, with two or three slices of salt pork; place a few thin slices of your paste here and there; drop in an egg or two if you have plenty. Fill the pan with flour and water, seasoned with a little pepper and salt. If the meat be very lean, put in a piece of butter, or such sweet gravies as you may happen to have. Cover the top with crust, and put it in the oven, or bake-kettle, to cook half an hour, or an hour, according to the size of the pie. Some people think this the nicest way of cooking fresh chickens. When thus cooked, they should be parboiled before they are put into the pan, and the water they are boiled in should be added. A chicken pie needs to be cooked an hour and a half, if parboiled; two hours if not."

—*The American Frugal Housewife*, 1832

Modern Method:

1. Make piecrust: Measure flour into bowl. Using your hand, rub lard or shortening into flour, working until well blended. Make a depression in the center of this mixture, pour in water and mix rapidly by hand to blend. Divide this dough to make two 9-inch crusts. Roll out one ball of dough to line pie plate with crust. Trim strips of dough from around edges and reserve.

2. Layer chopped meat and pork in piecrust. Put trimmed scraps of piecrust in around the edges. If broth is used instead of gravy, sprinkle ¼ cup flour over top of filling.

3. Beat eggs with a fork, and combine with gravy or broth. Add salt and pepper to taste. Pour mixture over filling.

4. Cover pie with remaining crust; prick with a fork.

5. Bake 40 minutes at 375°F or until top is browned.

Hearth Method:

1. Preheat bake-oven or prepare coals if Dutch oven is used.

2. Follow Steps 1–4 in the Modern Method recipe.

3. Bake 1 hour, or a little less in Dutch oven.

Yield: 6 servings

Fried Fish

Fresh or frozen fish, whole or filleted

White cornmeal

2–4 ounces salt pork, bacon drippings, or fat reserved from another fish fry

"Cod has white stripes, and a haddock black stripes; they may be known apart by this. Haddock is the best for frying and cod is the best for boiling, or for a chowder. A thin tail is a sign of a poor fish; always choose a thick fish.

"When you are buying a mackerel, pinch the belly to ascertain whether it is good. If it gives under your finger, like a bladder half filled with wind, the fish is poor; if it feels hard like butter, the fish is good. It is cheaper to buy one large mackerel for ninepence, than two for four pence half-penny each.

"Fish should not be put in to fry until the fat is boiling hot; it is very necessary to observe this. It should be dipped in Indian meal before it is put in; and the skinny side uppermost, when first put in to prevent its breaking. It relishes better to be fried after salt pork, than to be fried in lard alone."

—*The American Frugal Housewife,* 1832

Modern Method:

1. Cut salt pork into small, thick strips and render fat for frying the fish.
2. Wash the fish and coat with cornmeal.
3. Place prepared fish into sizzling fat. Cook the fish 3–5 minutes on each side, turning once.

Hearth Method:

1. Follow Steps 1 and 2 in the Modern Method recipe, using either a hanging skillet or spider over coals.
2. Fish will cook more rapidly in a hanging skillet over a hot flame. If using a spider on a trivet, preheat spider over coals, and use fresh coals when fish is added and turned. Cook 8–10 minutes on each side.

Yield: 1 serving per ¾ pound of whole fish
  1 serving per ⅓ pound of fillet

Broiled Fish

"The fire for broiling fish must be very clear and the gridiron perfectly clean, which when hot, should be rubbed with a bit of suet. The fish, while broiling, must be often turned. Garnish with slices of lemon, finely scraped horseradish, fried oysters, smelts, whitings or strips of soles."

—The New England Economical Housekeeper, 1845

Suet

Fresh fish, whole, trimmed, or fish steak

Lemon slices, grated horseradish, fried oysters, smelts, or other small fish or fish slices for garnish

Modern Method:

1. Preheat broiler.
2. Grease broiling pan with suet before putting on the fish, skin-side down. Flat or thin fish should broil 2 inches from the heat for 3–4 minutes. They will not need to be turned. Thick and large pieces of fish should broil 6 inches from the heat for 5–6 minutes on each side.
3. Garnish on serving plate, as desired.

Hearth Method:

1. Preheat gridiron over hot coals and grease with suet.
2. Broil 4 minutes over hot coals.
3. Lift fish, grease gridiron, and turn fish to cook other side over fresh coals for 4 minutes.
4. Garnish on serving plate, as desired.

Yield: 1 serving per pound of whole fish
1 serving per ¾ pound trimmed fish
1 serving per ¼ pound fish steak

Codfish Cakes

1 cup leftover fish, mashed while still warm

½–1 cup mashed potatoes

1 egg

¼ cup bacon fat or other fat for frying

"Salt fish mashed with potatoes, with good butter or pork scraps to moisten it, is nicer the second day than it was the first. The fish should be minced very fine while it is warm. After it has gotten cold and dry it is difficult to do it nicely. There is no way of preparing salt fish for breakfast so nice as to roll it up in little balls, after it is mixed with mashed potatoes dip it into an egg, and fry it brown."

—*The American Frugal Housewife*, 1832

Modern Method:

1. Mash fish and potatoes together. Form into balls using about 1 teaspoon of mixture for each ball.
2. When ready to cook, roll balls in beaten egg to coat them.
3. Heat fat in a skillet. Add fish balls and fry for 10–15 minutes, to heat through, stirring frequently.

Hearth Method:

1. Follow Steps 1 and 2 in the recipe above.
2. Follow Step 3 in the recipe above, using a hanging skillet over hot coals.

"Codfish balls is a good dish for breakfast in the winter season."

—Sarah Josepha Hale,
The Way to Live Well and Be Well While We Live (Philadelphia, 1839)

Poached Fish

"A common sized cod-fish should be put in when the water is boiling hot, and boil about twenty minutes. Haddock is not as good for boiling as cod; it takes about the same time to boil.

"A piece of halibut which weighs four pounds is a large dinner for a family of six or seven. It should boil forty minutes. No fish put in till the water boils. Melted butter for sauce."

—The American Frugal Housewife, 1832

A large fillet of fish

Boiling water

2 tablespoons melted butter for each serving of fish, optional

A Most Delicious Salad Sauce, optional (recipe on page 72)

Modern Method:

1. Bring water to a boil in a large fish boiler or roasting pan.
2. Slip fish gently into the water and simmer 5–8 minutes per pound, depending on the thickness of the fish.
3. Serve with butter or A Most Delicious Salad Sauce.

Hearth Method:

Follow Steps 1–3 in the Modern Method recipe, using a large kettle or very deep skillet over moderate heat.

Yield: 2 servings per pound

Macaroni *(Homemade Noodles)*

4 eggs

2½ cups flour

½ teaspoon salt

"Beat four eggs for eight or ten minutes, strain them and stir in flour till stiff enough to work into a paste upon a marble or stone slab, add flour till it be a stiff paste, and work it well; cut off a small bit at a time, roll it out thin as paper, and cut it with a paste-cutter or knife into very narrow strips; twist and lay them down upon a clean cloth in a dry, warm place; in a few hours it will be perfectly dry and hard; put it into a box with white paper under and over it. It may be cut into small stars or circles to be used for soup and not require so much cooking as the Italian macaroni."

—The Housekeeper's Book, 1838

Modern and Hearth Methods:

1. Beat eggs. Put flour and salt into bowl and make a well in center of flour. Pour beaten eggs into well in flour and gently mix flour and eggs together, using your fingers. When lightly mixed, turn mixture onto floured board and knead for 10 minutes. (The kneading process may also be done in a food processor.)

2. Divide dough into six pieces. With rolling pin, roll into sheets of desired thickness. Slice with knife into desired width. Twist and place on towel to dry.

Yield: 6–8 servings

Macaroni with Parmesan Cheese

"Put a piece of butter, half a pound of macaroni, an onion stuck with two cloves, and a little salt into hot water, boil them for three quarters of an hour, and then, if the macaroni is flexible, take it out and drain it well. Put it into another saucepan with two ounces of butter, three of grated Parmesan cheese, a little pepper and nutmeg; toss up the whole together, adding two or three spoonfuls of cream; when done, put it on a dish, and serve it very hot."

—*The Housekeeper's Book*, 1838

8 ounces dry pasta (either broad egg noodles or fettucine)

1 small onion

2 cloves

1 teaspoon salt

4 tablespoons butter

1/3 cup parmesan cheese

1/4 teaspoon nutmeg

3 tablespoons cream

Modern Method:

1. Boil pasta until tender, according to directions, adding to water a small peeled onion with 2 cloves stuck into it, 1 teaspoon salt, and 1 tablespoon of butter.
2. Drain pasta and add remaining 3 tablespoons butter, cheese, pepper, nutmeg, and cream. Toss until well mixed.

Hearth Method:

1. Follow Step 1 in Modern Method recipe, using a large hanging pot.
2. Follow Step 2 in Modern Method recipe.

Yield: 4 side-dish servings

Dressed Macaroni

8 ounces macaroni

Chicken or beef broth for cooking macaroni

½ teaspoon salt

½ teaspoon mace

1½ cups grated cheese

½ cup fresh grated bread crumbs

¼ cup butter

"Simmer it in a little stock, with pounded mace and salt. When quite tender, take it out of the liquor, lay it in a dish; grate over it good deal of cheese, then over that put bread, grated very fine. Warm some butter without oiling, and pour it from a boat through a little earthen colander all over the crumbs, and brown the bread of a fine color. The bread should be in separate crumbs, and look light."

—*The Cook's Own Book*, 1832

Modern Method:
1. Prepare pasta according to directions, but using either chicken or beef broth with salt and mace instead of water. Drain.
2. Mix cooked pasta with cheese and put into greased baking dish. Cover with bread crumbs and drizzle with butter.
3. Bake in a 350°F oven for 20 minutes or until top is browned.

Hearth Method:
1. Prepare pasta as in Step 1 in Modern Method recipe, using a hanging kettle.
2. Mix cooked, drained pasta with cheese and place in greased redware baking dish. Cover with bread crumbs and drizzle with butter.
3. Preheat bake-kettle 15 minutes. Bake in preheated bake-kettle for 15–20 minutes or until top is light brown.

Yield: 4 side-dish servings

Peas

"Dried peas need not be soaked overnight. They should be stewed slowly four or five hours in considerable water with a piece of pork. The older beans and peas are, the longer they should cook."

—The American Frugal Housewife, 1832

1 pound dried peas

Water to cover peas

Meaty ham bone or ½ pound pork

Modern Method:

1. Combine peas, water, and bone or meat in a heavy pot with a lid.
2. Bring to a boil, reduce heat, and simmer 3–4 hours or until tender.

Hearth Method:

1. Follow Step 1 in the Modern Method recipe, using a hanging cooking pot with a cover.
2. Bring to a boil, reduce heat, and simmer 3–4 hours. Add more boiling water if necessary before peas are tender.

Yield: 8 cups

Omelet

8–10 eggs

1 tablespoon cold water

1 teaspoon salt

½ teaspoon pepper

3 tablespoons butter

OPTIONAL:
½ cup chopped fresh parsley

1 small chopped onion, fried until translucent

½ cup chopped cooked ham

½ cup chopped cooked tongue

¼ cup chopped cooked anchovy

½ dozen oysters, chopped and cooked

1 tablespoon chopped chives

"The following receipt is the basis of all omelets, of which you may make an endless variety. Break eight or ten eggs into a pan, add pepper, salt and a spoonful of cold water, beat them up with a whisk; in the meantime put some fresh butter into a frying pan, when it is quite melted and nearly boiling, put in the eggs, &c with a skimmer; as it is frying, take up the edges, that they may be properly done; when cooked, double it; serve very hot."

—*The Cook's Own Book,* 1832

Modern Method:

1. Beat eggs, water, salt, and pepper until well blended.
2. Add one or more desired optional ingredients.
3. Melt butter in a skillet.
4. Pour egg mixture into melted butter. As edges cook, lift them and tilt skillet to allow uncooked egg to run underneath, until the egg is firm.
5. When cooked, fold in half and flip on to a warm plate. Serve hot.

Hearth Method:

1. Follow Steps 1 and 2 in the Modern Method recipe.
2. Melt butter in a hanging skillet over a moderate to low fire.
3. Follow Steps 4 and 5 in the Modern Method recipe.

Yield: 6–8 servings

Potted Cheese

"Cut and pound four ounces of Cheshire cheese, one and a half of fine butter, a teaspoon of white pounded sugar, a little bit of mace and a glass of white wine. Press it down in a deep pot."

— *A New System of Domestic Cookery*, 1807

Modern Method:

Using either food processor or mixer, combine all ingredients (except crackers) until smooth. Adjust spice according to taste.

Hearth Method:

Combine all ingredients (except crackers) in large bowl, gently pounding with mortar until smooth.

Yield: 1½ cups

2 cups grated hard cheese (an assortment of cheddar and Romano)

2 ounces butter

2 teaspoons white sugar

1 teaspoon mace

¼ cup white port wine

Crackers or slice of bread to serve on

Roasted Cheese

1¼ cups grated cheddar or other hard cheese

2 hard-boiled egg yolks, mashed

2–3 cups soft bread crumbs

4 tablespoons butter

1 tablespoon mustard

Dash of salt and pepper

8 slices lightly toasted bread, or rusks (recipe on page 190)

"Grate three ounces of fat cheese, mix it with the yolks of two eggs, four ounces of grated bread and three ounces of butter; beat the whole well in a mortar with a dessert spoonful of mustard and a little salt and pepper. Toast some bread, cut it into proper pieces; lay the paste, as above, thick upon them, put them into a Dutch oven covered with a dish till hot through, remove the dish and let the cheese brown a little. Serve as hot as possible."

—*A New System of Domestic Cookery,* 1807

Modern Method:

1. Blend cheese, mashed egg yolks, bread crumbs, butter, mustard, salt, and pepper.
2. Spread paste on toast. Bake in 350°F oven covered for 15 minutes. Remove cover for last 5 minutes to brown the cheese.

Hearth Method:

1. Follow Step 1 in the Modern Method recipe.
2. Spread paste on toast. Place on pie plate covered with a plate in a Dutch oven. Place coals below Dutch oven and on the lid.
3. Bake 15 minutes. Remove cover from pie plate. Re-cover Dutch oven, heap fresh coals on cover for 5 minutes while cheese browns.

Yield: 4 servings

Pounded Cheese

"Cut a pound of good mellow Cheddar, Cheshire, or North Wiltshire cheese into thin bits, add to it two, and if the Cheese is dry, three ounces of fresh butter, pound and rub them well together in a mortar till it is quite smooth.

"Obs.—When cheese is dry, and for those whose digestion is feeble, this is the best way of eating it and spread it on Bread, it makes an excellent Luncheon or Supper.

"N.B. The piquance of this buttery, caseous relish, is sometimes increased by pounding with it Curry Powder, Ground Spice, Cayenne Pepper, and a little made mustard; and some moisten it with a glass of Sherry.

"If pressed down hard in a jar, and covered with clarified butter, it will keep for several days in cool weather."

—*The Cook's Oracle*, 1823

2 cups grated cheese (assorted hard, sharp cheeses such as cheddar and Romano)

¼ cup butter

2 teaspoons made mustard (see recipe page 108)

¼ teaspoon cayenne pepper

1 teaspoon curry powder

1 tablespoon sherry

Note: The English regional cheeses named in this recipe give away its origin.

Modern Method:

Using either food processor or mixer, combine all ingredients until smooth. Adjust spice according to taste.

Hearth Method:

Combine all ingredients in large bowl, gently pounding with mortar until smooth.

Yield: 1½ cups of spread

A Most Delicious Salad Sauce

4 hard–boiled egg yolks

1 teaspoon salt

2 tablespoons prepared mustard (recipe on page 108)

6 tablespoons vegetable oil

1 teaspoon Worcestershire sauce, optional

¼ cup cream or whole milk

6 teaspoons vinegar

"Take the yolks of four hard-boiled eggs, rub them through a sieve, and add to them one teaspoonful of salt, stir well up, then add two tablespoonsful of made mustard, stir well up, then add by one spoonful at each time, six spoonsful of salad oil; mix this well together until it becomes as smooth as mustard, then put in one teaspoonful of anchovy sauce, and one gill of cream or new milk, and stir well together; and last of all put in by degrees some good vinegar to your own taste. Should you make it too sharp with vinegar, add one teaspoonful of fine white sugar in powder, this will soften it, and give it an excellent flavour. Bottle it for use. This will keep for any length of time in the hottest weather and is excellent with any kind of salad or boiled slaw, and is a fine relish with fish. Shake it well up before you put it on your salad."

—The House Servant's Directory, 1827

Modern and Hearth Methods:
1. Force the egg yolks through a strainer or grater.
2. Add salt and mustard, mix well.
3. Add oil, 1 tablespoonful at a time, blending between each addition.
4. Add anchovy sauce, if desired.
5. Add cream or milk and blend well.
6. Add vinegar 2 teaspoonfuls at a time.

Yield: 1 cup

Vegetables

Cooking Vegetables

"Put in no green vegetables till the water boils if you would keep all their sweetness. Asparagus should be boiled fifteen or twenty minutes; half an hour if old. Beets need to be boiled an hour and a half. Beet tops should be boiled twenty minutes. String beans should be boiled from twenty minutes to sixty, according to their age. Cabbages need to be boiled an hour. Corn should be boiled from twenty minutes to forty, according to age. Dandelions should be boiled half an hour or three quarters, according to age. Green peas should be boiled from twenty minutes to sixty, according to their age. Spinach should be boiled three or four minutes. . . . The lower part of a squash should be boiled half an hour and the neck pieces fifteen or twenty minutes longer."

—*The American Frugal Housewife*, 1832

Note: Vegetables today are preferred crisp-tender rather than "boiled to rags" as they would be if Mrs. Child's instructions were followed to the minute on a stove.

Modern Method:

1. Prepare vegetables for cooking.
2. Boil water in a large saucepan. Add vegetables. Simmer, covered, until tender.

Asparagus: no more than 15 minutes.

Beans: about 20 minutes.

Beets: ½ hour to 1 hour for young beets; they should be tender when pierced with a fork. 1–2 hours for old, large beets.

Greens: 20 minutes.

Cabbage: The old way was to cut into sections and boil for a long period. Instead, shred cabbage and boil 5 minutes.

Corn: Mrs. Child gives the timing for old-fashioned varieties of flint corn, grown for corn meal, rather than varieties of sweet corn. Sweet corn should be boiled or steamed 4–10 minutes.

Dandelions and other wild and edible greens: 35–40 minutes.

Peas: 10–15 minutes.

Squash: Put the neck pieces in a large pot of boiling water. Turn down heat and simmer for 15 minutes. Add remaining squash and cook 30 minutes, or until tender. Small pieces will cook more rapidly.

Hearth Method:

1. Follow Step 1 in the Modern Method recipe.

2. Boil water in a hanging iron pot. Add vegetables and return pot to moderate fire. Simmer covered until tender.

3. Follow cooking times given in the Modern Method recipe.

Onions

1 pound onions, white or brown, skinned

1¼ cups milk

2 tablespoons butter

1 teaspoon salt

1 teaspoon pepper

"It is a good plan to boil onions in milk and water, it diminishes the strong taste of that vegetable. It is an excellent way of serving up onions, to chop them after they are boiled, and put them in a stewpan, with a little milk, butter, salt and pepper and let them stew about fifteen minutes. This gives them a fine flavor and they can be served up very hot."

—*The American Frugal Housewife,* 1832

Modern Method:

1. Peel onions. Cook whole in 1 inch of boiling water and ¼ cup milk.
2. Pierce onions with fork. When almost tender, after about 20 minutes, remove from heat and drain.
3. Chop onions and return to heat in a clean pan, with remaining milk, butter, salt, and pepper. Simmer 15 minutes.

Hearth Method:

1. Follow Step 1 in the Modern Method recipe, using a hanging pot.
2. Follow Step 2 in the Modern Method recipe, removing pot from fire to check the onions for tenderness.
3. Chop onions. Wipe out pot or rinse with hot water. Return to cooking pot with butter, milk, salt, and pepper. Simmer for 15 minutes.

Yield: 4 servings

Potatoes

"New potatoes should boil fifteen or twenty minutes, three quarters of an hour or an hour is not too much for large old potatoes; common sized ones half an hour. If you wish to have potatoes mealy, do not let them stop boiling for an instant and when they are done, turn the water off and let them steam for ten or twelve minutes over the fire. See they don't stay long enough to burn to the kettle. In Canada they cut the skin all off and put them in pans to be cooked over a stove by steam. Those who have eaten them, say they are mealy and white, looking like large snow-balls when brought upon the table."

—*The American Frugal Housewife,* 1832

Modern Method:

1. Wash potatoes well; do not peel or cut up.

2. Put potatoes into a heavy saucepan with a lid, and cover them with cold water. Bring to a boil, reduce heat, and cook 20–30 minutes or until almost soft. Time will depend on size of potato.

3. Pour off all the water and re-cover saucepan. Let potatoes steam for 15 minutes, or until rest of meal is ready. Remove skins before serving, if desired.

Hearth Method:

1. Follow Step 1 in the Modern Method recipe.

2. Put potatoes into a large hanging pot with a lid, and cover them with cold water. Bring to a boil directly over fire, cooking for about 20–30 minutes or until almost soft. Time will depend on size of potato.

3. Pour off the water. Put a clean cloth over potatoes, cover the pan, and set it beside fire to steam for 15 minutes or until rest of meal is ready.

4. Remove skins before serving, if desired.

Yield: 1 serving per potato

Fried Potatoes

Potatoes

Butter or other fat for frying

Thinned pancake batter, optional (recipe on page 166)

"To fry potatoes take the skin off raw potatoes, slice and fry them, either in butter or thin batter."

—A New System of Domestic Cookery, 1807

Modern Method:

1. Peel raw potatoes. Cut into thin slices.
2. Melt butter and add potatoes plain or after dipping in a thin pancake batter.
3. Fry 15–20 minutes or until crisp and brown.

Hearth Method:

Follow Steps 1–3 in the Modern Method recipe, using a hanging skillet over a hot fire.

"The mechanics and manufacturers of the United States—their success or failure will be the barometer of our Nation's strength; if they fall not alone."

—Ladies' Mirror (July, 1833)

Broiled Potatoes

"Parboil, then slice and broil them. Or parboil, and then set them whole on the gridiron over a very small fire, and when thoroughly done, send them up with their skins on."

—A New System of Domestic Cookery, 1807

Potatoes, of roughly equal size for convenience in cooking

Modern Method:

1. Bring a large pot of water to a boil. Add unpeeled potatoes individually, to keep water boiling. Cook for 10 minutes.

2. Cut potatoes into thick slices or leave them whole, if small.

3. Arrange on broiler or grill and broil 10 minutes on each side.

Hearth Method:

1. Follow Steps 1 and 2 in the Modern Method recipe.

2. Arrange on a gridiron, place over a slow fire, and grill until crispy, 15 minutes or more depending on heat of coals beneath the gridiron.

Yield: 1 serving per potato

Mashed Potatoes

4–6 potatoes, boiled in their jackets

1 cup milk

½ cup butter

Salt to taste

"Boil, peel and break to paste the potatoes; then to two pounds, add a quarter of a pint of milk and a little salt with two or three ounces of butter and stir all well over the fire. Serve in this manner; or when placed in a dish in a form, then brown the top with a salamander."
—A New System of Domestic Cookery, 1807

Note: A *salamander* is a circular iron plate that is heated and placed on top of a dish of food to be browned. An 1815 cookbook notes that "a kitchen shovel is sometimes substituted for it."

Modern Method:

1. Peel potatoes and mash well.
2: Add milk, butter, and a little salt and mix well.
3. If a browned top is desired, place pan under broiler for 10–15 minutes or until browned.

Hearth Method:

1. Follow Steps 1 and 2 in the Modern Method recipe.
2. If a browned top is desired, place in a heat-proof dish and use a preheated salamander or put into a preheated bake-kettle, cover and add coals to brown in about 10 minutes.

Yield: 4 servings

Potato Eggs

"Mash perfectly smooth six or seven boiled potatoes, add a piece of butter the size of a walnut, the beaten yolk of an egg, half an onion pounded, a little boiled minced parsley, some pepper and salt; make it into the form of small eggs or pears, roll them into a well-beaten egg, and then into grated bread seasoned with pepper and salt, fry them in plenty of lard or drippings till they are of a fine brown colour, lay them before the fire to drain; serve them with a fringe of fried parsley."

—*The Practice of Cookery*, 1830

2 pounds potatoes, or about 6 or 7 medium ones

1 tablespoon butter

1 egg yolk

1 medium onion, chopped fine

4 teaspoons dried parsley (or ½ cup fresh chopped herbs)

Salt and pepper to taste

1 beaten egg

Bread crumbs seasoned with salt and pepper

Fat or drippings for frying

Modern Method:

1. Cook and mash potatoes.
2. Add butter and egg yolk to mashed potatoes and blend well.
3. Add herbs, chopped onion, salt, and pepper to taste; blend well.
4. Roll into balls, bite size if for hors d'oeuvres, larger if to be served with a meal.
5. Roll in beaten egg and then in bread crumbs.
6. Preheat frying pan with ½ inch of fat. Add potato balls and fry until browned and heated through.

Hearth Method:

1. Follow Steps 1–5 of Modern Method recipe.
2. Fry in ½ inch of fat in a hanging skillet or spider over hot coals, until browned or heated through, or place in a Dutch oven for 45 minutes with coals above and below.

Yield: 8 servings

Roast Potatoes under Meat

Potatoes, of roughly equal
size for convenience in
cooking

*"After being boiled, lay them on a dish, and place it in the dripping pan, baste them now and
then with a little of the meat dripping, and when one side is browned, turn the other; they
should all be of an equal colour."*

—*The Practice of Cookery*, 1830

Modern Method:

1. Bring a large pot of water to a boil and add unpeeled potatoes individually, to
keep water boiling. Cook for 10 minutes.
2. Add to pan in which beef or pork is roasting for last ½ hour of roasting time,
and baste with pan juices. Turn after 15 minutes.

Hearth Method:

1. Follow Step 1 in the Modern Method recipe, using a large hanging pot.
2. Place under roasting meat in reflector oven for last 30–40 minutes of cooking.
Turn after 15–20 minutes.

Yield: 1 serving per potato

Pickled Beet-Root

"Boil the roots tender, peel and cut them in what shape you please. Put them into a jar and pour over them a hot pickle of vinegar, pepper, ginger, and sliced horseradish. You may add capsicums and cayenne."

—*The Cook's Own Book,* 1832

2 pounds beets

Water to cover beets

1 cup vinegar

8 peppercorns

½ teaspoon ginger

1 tablespoon horseradish

½ teaspoon allspice or cayenne pepper, optional

Modern Method:

1. Cut tops off beets, leaving one inch of stem. Wash carefully. Put in saucepan, and half cover beets with water. Cover pan.

2. Cook until tender, ¾ hour for young beets, 1–2 hours for large, older beets.

3. Pierce beets with fork. When tender, remove from heat, peel and slice.

4. To prepare the pickle, combine 1 cup cooking liquid, vinegar, peppercorns, ginger, horseradish, and, if desired, allspice or cayenne pepper in a small pan. Bring to a boil, and pour over sliced beets. Discard remainder of cooking liquid.

5. Refrigerate 24 hours before serving to allow flavors to blend.

Hearth Method:

1. Follow Step 1 in the Modern Method recipe, using an uncovered hanging kettle over moderate fire. Add more boiling water, if necessary to keep beets covered. Follow Steps 2 and 3 in the Modern Method recipe, removing kettle from fire to check the beets for tenderness.

3. Follow Step 4 in the Modern Method recipe, using a small tin pan on a trivet over coals.

4. Follow Step 5 in the Modern Method recipe.

Yield: 8 servings

Stewed Tomatoes

6 large tomatoes

1 quart boiling water

1 tablespoon water

1 tablespoon butter

1 teaspoon salt

"Tomatoes should be skinned by pouring boiling water over them. After they are skinned, they should be stewed half an hour, in tin (not cast iron, to avoid harmful interaction of the acids with iron), with a little salt, a small bit of butter and a spoonful of water to keep them from burning. This is a delicious vegetable. It is easily cultivated and yields a most abundant crop."

—The American Frugal Housewife, 1832

Modern Method:

1. Place tomatoes in a bowl. Cover with boiling water. In a minute or two, the skins will slip off. Chop tomatoes.
2. Place in a saucepan with 1 tablespoon of water and the butter and salt. Heat slowly, stirring occasionally, until cooked through, about 20 minutes.

Hearth Method:

1. Follow Step 1 in the Modern Method recipe.
2. If you have a tin-lined hanging pot use it, or else use a metal pan on a trivet over coals to stew tomatoes with water, butter, and salt. Tomatoes will cook in 20–30 minutes.

Yield: 2 cups

Fricasseed Jerusalem Artichokes

"Wash and scrape or pare them: boil them in milk and water till they are soft, which will be from a quarter to a half of an hour. Take them out and stew them a few minutes in the following sauce: Roll a bit of butter, the size of a walnut, in flour, mix it with a half a pint of cream or milk; season it with pepper, salt and grated nutmeg."

—The Practice of Cookery, 1830

1 pound Jerusalem artichokes

1 cup milk

1 cup water

1 tablespoon butter

1 tablespoons flour

½ cup cream

½ teaspoon pepper

½ teaspoon nutmeg

Salt to taste

Note: Jerusalem artichokes are knobby tubers related to the North American sunflower. Not associated with Jerusalem, the name is probably derived from a corruption of *girasole,* Italian for sunflower.

Modern Method:

1. Wash Jerusalem artichokes and pare if needed. Boil in milk combined with water until tender, about 20 minutes. Drain.
2. Roll butter into flour. Warm cream over low heat. Add butter and flour mixture to cream, whisking to dissolve. Stir until it thickens.
3. Season with pepper, nutmeg, and salt. Add Jerusalem artichokes to sauce and serve.

Hearth Method:

1. Follow Step 1 in the Modern Method, using hanging kettle to boil.
2. Roll butter into flour. Heat cream in a redware bowl set on a trivet over hot coals. Add butter and flour mixture to cream, whisking to dissolve. Stir until it thickens.
3. Season with pepper, nutmeg, and salt. Add Jerusalem artichokes to sauce and serve.

Yield: 4 servings

Cold Slaw and Hot Slaw

1 head (2 pounds) cabbage

½ cup butter

½ cup cider vinegar

1 teaspoon salt

1½ teaspoon pepper

"Cold Slaw. Select the hardest, firmest head of cabbage. Cut it in two, and shave it as fine as possible. A cabbage cutter is best. It must be done evenly and nicely. Lay it on a nice deep dish. Melt together vinegar, a small piece of butter, pepper, a little salt. Let it scald and pour it over.

"Hot Slaw. This is made in the same manner, except it is laid in a sauce pan with the dressing, and just scalded, but not baked. Send it to the table hot."

—*The Skilful Housewife's Book,* 1846

Modern Method:

1. Shave cabbage very thin, cutting out core.
2. In large pot, scald together butter, cider vinegar, salt, and pepper.
3. For hot slaw: Add cabbage to hot mixture and cook over moderate heat, stirring frequently until just tender, about 10–15 minutes. (For cold slaw: Prepare dressing as directed. Toss shaved cabbage with warm dressing.)

Hearth Method:

1. Follow Step 1 in the Modern Method recipe.
2. Heat butter, vinegar, salt, and pepper in hanging kettle.
3. Follow Step 3 in the Modern Method recipe.

Yield: 6–8 servings

Fried Cucumbers

"When pared, cut them in slices as thick as a dollar. Dry them with a cloth, and season with pepper and salt, and sprinkle them with flour. Have butter hot and lay them in. Fry of a light brown and send them to the table hot. They make a breakfast dish."

—The Skilful Housewife's Book, 1846

4 pickling cucumbers (about 4 cups when sliced)

1 teaspoon salt

1 teaspoon pepper

1/3 cup flour

1/2 cup butter

Modern Method:

1. Cut unpeeled cucumbers into 1/4-inch slices. Lay on a towel and pat dry.

2. Sprinkle with salt and pepper. Lightly coat seasoned cucumber slices with flour.

3. Melt part of butter in frying pan and fry cucumbers until light brown, about 10–15 minutes, turning halfway through cooking time. When browned, transfer to a heated serving dish and keep warm. Add more butter to frying pan and continue to cook until remaining slices are prepared.

Hearth Method:

Follow Steps 1–3 in the Modern Method recipe, using a hanging skillet or spider over hot coals.

Yield: 4–6 servings

Fried Parsnips

1 pound parsnips

Salt and pepper to taste

¼ cup butter or lard

"Those that have remained in the ground till March are usually very fine. Boil them an hour and a half, and cook enough for two days. Scrape the outside, split them, and lay them on a dish with a little butter, salt and pepper. Take those that are left the next day, and lay them on a hot griddle or spider, with a little butter, ham fat, or nice drippings and brown them. These are better than on the first day. Brown them when first boiled if you choose."

—The Young Housekeeper's Friend, 1846

Modern Method:

1. Scrub parsnips well with vegetable brush. Cook in boiling water until fork tender, about 20 minutes for medium-size parsnips, 35–40 minutes for large parsnips.
2. Cut in quarters lengthwise and season with salt and pepper.
3. Heat fat in frying pan and fry parsnips until golden brown, about 10–15 minutes.

Hearth Method:

1. Follow Steps 1 and 2 in the Modern Method recipe, boiling in a hanging kettle.
2. Fry parsnips in hot fat in a hanging skillet or in a spider over hot coals until golden brown, about 10–15 minutes.

Yield: 4–6 servings

Turnip Sauce

"Boil your turnips and mash them fine; add the same amount of mealy mashed potatoes, season with salt and pepper, moisten it with cream or butter."

—*The New England Economical Housekeeper,* 1845

Note: The term sauce often referred to a medley of vegetables cooked together, rather than the modern reference to thickened liquid.

Modern Method:

1. In large pot, boil turnips until fork tender, about 20 minutes.
2. Add potatoes to pot with turnips and continue to boil until potatoes are tender, checking to maintain water level.
3. Drain potatoes and turnips.
4. Mash well. Add cream, butter and salt to taste.

Hearth Method:

Follow Steps 1–4 in the Modern Method recipe, boiling in hanging kettle over the fire.

Yield: 6 servings

3 small white turnips, peeled and chopped

3 medium potatoes, peeled and chopped

1 cup cream

½ cup butter

Salt to taste

Stewed Beets

2 pounds beets

Water to cover beets

2 tablespoon butter

1 tablespoon flour

2 medium onions, par-boiled

2 tablespoon chopped parsley

½ cup cider vinegar

Salt

Pepper

"Boil them first, and then scrape and slice them. Put them into a stew-pan with a piece of butter rolled in flour, some boiled onion and parsley chopped fine, and a little vinegar, salt and pepper. Set the pan on hot coals, and let the beets stew for a quarter of an hour."

—Directions for Cookery, 1851

Modern Method:

1. Cut tops off beets, leaving 1 inch of stem. Wash carefully. Put beets in saucepan and cover with water.

2. Boil until tender, ¾ hour for young beets, 1–2 hours for large, older beets.

3. While beets are cooking, mix together butter and flour. Chop onion and parsley (if using fresh). Set aside.

4. Pierce beets with fork. When tender, remove from water, discarding cooking water. Place beets in container of cold water. Gently rub off peels and slice. Return sliced beets to pan.

5. Add butter mixture to warm beets and mix thoroughly. Stir in vinegar, onion and parsley. Add salt and pepper to taste. Cook for 5 minutes or until sauce thickens.

Hearth Method:

1. Follow Steps 1–3 in the Modern Method recipe, using a hanging kettle over the fire.

2. Follow Steps 4 and 5 in the Modern Method, using a redware bowl on a trivet over hot coals instead of the kettle to heat and thicken sauce.

Yield: 8 servings

Soups

Beef Soup

5–6 pounds beef bones—
for richer flavor, use a
combination of bones with
meat: shank, short ribs, or
bones from which a roast has
been carved

4 quarts water

6–8 medium to large onions

1 cup flour

2 cups water

1 teaspoon salt

1 teaspoon pepper

¾ cup catsup, optional
(recipe on page 200)

1 sliced lemon, optional

Crackers or cubed crusts or
toasted bread

DUMPLINGS:
1 egg

¼ cup milk

1 cup flour

"Beef soup should be stewed four hours over a slow fire. Just water enough to keep the meat covered. If you have any bones left of roast meat, &c. it is a good plan to boil them with the meat, and take them out half an hour before the soup is done. A pint of flour and water, with salt, pepper, twelve or sixteen onions, should be put in twenty minutes before the soup is done. Be careful and do not throw in salt and pepper too plentifully; it is easy to add to it, and not easy to diminish. A lemon, cut up and put in half an hour before it is done, adds to the flavor. If you have tomato catsup in the house, a cupful will make soup rich. Some people put in crackers, some thin slices of crust, made nearly as short as common shortcake; and some stir up two or three eggs with milk and flour, and drop it in with a spoon."

—*The American Frugal Housewife*, 1832

Note: The word *catsup* (or ketchup) is derived from Chinese *ketsiap*, meaning fermented fish sauce, as well as the Malay word *kechap*. The Beef Soup recipe specifies tomato catsup in order to distinguish it from other common catsups in the nineteenth century such as anchovy, mushroom, or walnut.

Modern Method:

1. Place the beef bones in a large stockpot and cover with water. Simmer slowly, uncovered, for 2–3 hours.
2. Remove meat from bones and cut it up. Discard bones.
3. Put meat and broth back into saucepan and return to heat. There will be about 2 quarts of broth. Add onions, whole or chopped. To thicken, make a paste of the flour and water and stir gradually into soup. Simmer 15 minutes. Season with salt and pepper, add catsup or lemon, or make dumplings, if desired.

4. To make dumplings, beat together egg and milk. Stir in flour until blended. Drop batter by spoonfuls into pot of soup to simmer during last half hour of cooking.

5. Serve soup with crackers or cubed crusts or toasted bread.

Hearth Method:

1. Place the beef bones in a large hanging kettle, cover with water. Bring to boil over a hot fire, then remove from hottest fire, or let it die back, while contents of pot simmer for 3½ hours.

2. Follow Steps 2 and 3 in the Modern Method recipe, over hot fire.

3. Follow Steps 4 and 5 in the Modern Method recipe.

Yield: 10–12 servings

Fish Chowder

4 large potatoes

4 large onions

4 pounds fish

12 common crackers

6 slices salt pork

4 teaspoons salt

4 teaspoons pepper

⅓ cup flour

4–5 cups water

For a different flavor, add one-quarter of the following with each layer:

Sliced lemon

1 cup catsup (recipe on page 200)

1 dozen cooked clams

1 cup dark beer

"Four pounds of fish are enough to make a chowder for four or five people; half a dozen slices of salt pork in the bottom of the pot; hang it high, so that the pork may not burn; take it out when done very brown; put in a layer of fish, cut in lengthwise slices, then a layer formed of crackers, small or sliced onions, and potatoes sliced as thin as a four-pence, mixed with pieces of pork you have fried; then a layer of fish again, and so on. Six crackers are enough. Strew a little salt and pepper over each layer; over the whole pour a bowl-full of flour and water, enough to come up even with the surface of what you have in the pot. A sliced lemon adds to the flavor. A cup of tomato catsup is very excellent. Some people put in a cup of beer. A few clams are a pleasant addition. It should be covered so as not to let a particle of steam escape, if possible. Do not open it, except when nearly done, to taste if it be well seasoned."

—The American Frugal Housewife, 1832

Note: The term *chowder* is most likely derived from the French word *chaudiere*, referring to a form of an iron kettle.

Modern Method:

1. Cut potatoes and onions into thin slices, slice fish, and split crackers.
2. Using a large heavy kettle, fry slices of salt pork until browned and remove crisped pork.
3. Leave fat in kettle. Build the first layer with 1 pound of fish; one-quarter of the sliced potatoes, onions, pork scraps, and split crackers; 1 teaspoon of salt; 1 teaspoon of pepper. Repeat until all ingredients are layered in soup kettle.
4. Blend flour and 1 cup of water to make a smooth paste. Stir in remaining water and pour this mixture over fish layers until covered.
5. Cover the pot and heat slowly until contents simmer. In 30–45 minutes, remove the lid to test that the potatoes are done, and correct the seasonings, if necessary.

Hearth Method:

1. Follow Step 1 of the Modern Method recipe.

2. Follow Step 2 of the Modern Method recipe, using a large hanging pot over moderate heat.

3. Follow Steps 3 and 4 of the Modern Method recipe.

4. Cover the pot with a pie plate or foil, if it does not have a lid. Heat over moderate fire for 30–45 minutes, remove the lid to test that the potatoes are done, and correct the seasonings, if necessary.

Yield: 4–5 servings

Clams with Broth

3–4 dozen clams, in shells, 6–8 per person

Water to cover bottom of cooking pot

¼ cup of flour

¼ cup of butter or cream

Pepper and vinegar to taste

6 slices of toast or 6 common crackers split in half

"Clams should boil about fifteen minutes in their own water; no other need be added except a spoonful to keep the bottom shells from burning. It is easy to tell when they are done, by the shells starting wide open. After they are done, they should be taken from the shells, washed thoroughly in their own water, and put in a stewing pan. The water should then be strained through a cloth, so as to get out all the grit; the clams should be simmered in it ten or fifteen minutes; a little thickening of flour and water added; half a dozen slices of toasted bread or cracker; and pepper, vinegar and butter to your taste. Salt is not needed."

—*The American Frugal Housewife*, 1832

Modern Method:

1. Cover bottom of pot with ½ inch of water to prevent clams on the bottom from burning.
2. Add clams and boil 15 minutes or until all shells open.
3. Remove clams from pot and shell. Rinse clams thoroughly in water in which they were cooked. Strain this water through cheesecloth to remove grit. Clean cooking pot.
4. Return clams and strained water to pot. Stir in paste of flour and butter or cream and bring almost to a boil.
5. Add pepper and vinegar to taste. Serve with toast or crackers.

Hearth Method:

1. Cover bottom of hanging kettle with ½ inch of water.
2. Add clams and hang over moderate to high heat. Boil 15 minutes or until all shells are open. Remove pot from fire.
3. Follow Step 3 in the Modern Method recipe.
4. Return clams and strained water to pot. Stir in paste made of flour and butter or cream. Hang over moderate fire 15 minutes or until it almost comes to the boil.
5. Follow Step 5 in the Modern Method recipe.

Yield: 6 servings

Gourd Soup

"Should be made of full-grown gourds but not those that have hard skins; slice three or four and put them in a stewpan, with two or three onions, and a good bit of butter; set them over a slow fire till quite tender (be careful not to let them burn); then add two ounces of crust of bread and two quarts of good consommé, season with salt and cayenne pepper; boil ten minutes or a quarter of an hour; skim off all the fat, and pass it through a tamis; then make it quite hot, and serve up with fried bread."

—The Cook's Own Book, 1832.

3 onions

4–5 pounds butternut squash

¼ pound butter

2 quarts either beef or chicken broth

½ loaf of stale, crusty bread

Cayenne pepper

Salt

Additional butter or oil for frying bread

Note: The term *gourd* in this recipe refers to squash. A *tamis* is a fine sieve, used to puree the soup before serving.

Modern Method:

1. Peel and slice onions and squash.
2. Melt ¼ pound butter in soup pot. Sauté onions and squash in butter until tender, stirring frequently.
3. Cover with broth and simmer until squash and onions are very tender.
4. While soup is simmering, grate 1 cup bread crumbs from loaf. Cut remaining bread into cubes and fry in butter or oil in batches.
5. Just before serving, press soup through colander or sieve to puree. Thicken with bread crumbs. Add salt and cayenne pepper (careful not to add too much cayenne!) to taste.
6. Serve with 3–4 pieces of fried bread on top.

Hearth Method:

1. Follow Steps 1–3 in the Modern Method recipe, using a large hanging pot over moderate heat.
2. Follow Steps 4–6 in the Modern Method recipe, using a hanging skillet to fry the bread cubes.

Yield: 8 servings

Turnip Soup

12 small purple-top turnips

½ gallon water

1 teaspoon black pepper

2 onions, 1 large and 1 small

6 whole cloves

⅛ teaspoon mace

¼ teaspoon nutmeg

Herbs of your choice

6 stalks celery

2 carrots

2 tablespoon flour

Butter for frying

1 cup vermicelli, optional

Salt

"To make Turnip Soup pear [pare] a bunch of turnips (save out three or four) put them into a gallon of water with half an ounce of black pepper, an onion stuck with cloves, three blades of mace, half a nutmeg bruised, a good bunch of sweet herbs, and a large crust of bread. Boil them an hour and a half, then pass them through a sieve; clean a bunch of celery, cut it small and put it into your turnips and liquor with two of the turnips you saved and two young carrots cut in dice; cover it close and let it stew; then cut two turnips and carrots in dice, flour them, and fry them brown in butter with two large onions cut thin and fried likewise, put them all into your soup with some vermacelli. Let it boil softly until your celery is tender and your soup is good. Season it with salt to your palate."

—*New England Cookery,* 1808

Modern Method:

1. Peel turnips. Cut 4 small turnips into pieces and put in kettle with water, pepper, small onion stuck with cloves, mace, nutmeg, and herbs. Simmer for 1½ hours.
2. Puree boiled turnips in a blender or food mill.
3. Put the turnip puree into pot along with diced celery, 1 diced large turnip, and 1 diced carrot. Simmer for 20 minutes.
4. Dice remaining turnips and carrot, coat with flour, and fry in butter. Slice and fry large onion. Add sautéed vegetables and vermicelli, if desired, to simmering ingredients and cook until celery is tender, about 20 minutes. Salt to taste.

Hearth Method:

1. Follow Step 1 in the Modern Method recipe, using a large hanging pot over high heat. When water boils, allow fire to become moderate to simmer vegetables.
2. Mash turnips with a wooden masher or a fork.
3. Follow Step 3 in the Modern Method recipe, over a very moderate fire.
4. Follow Step 4 in the Modern Method recipe, using a hanging skillet or in a spider over coals drawn out on the hearth.

Yield: 10 servings

Onion Soup

"Take half a pound of Butter, put it into a Stew pan and set it on the fire, and let all the Butter melt, and boil untill it is done making a Noise; then have ready ten or a Dozen middling sized Onions, peeled and cut small, which throw into the Butter, and let them fry for a Quarter of an hour; then shake in a little Flour, and stir them round; shake your Pan and let them do a few minutes longer; when you must pour in a Quart or three Pints of boiling water; stir them round, and throw in a good piece of the upper Crust of the stalest Bread you have. Season with Salt to your Palate. Let it then stew or boil gently for ten Minutes observing to stir it often; after which take it off the Fire, and have ready the yolks of two Eggs beaten fine in a Spoonful of Vinegar, and then stir it gently and by Degrees into your Soup, mixing it well. This is a delicious Dish."

—*Mrs. Gardiner's Receipts,* 1763

¼ pound butter

10 medium onions, peeled and sliced thin

4 tablespoons flour

2 quarts boiling water

2 tablespoons salt

1 teaspoon pepper

Slice of bread

2 egg yolks

2 teaspoons vinegar

Modern Method:

1. Melt butter in a large soup pot, add sliced onions, and fry gently for 15 minutes. Onions should be translucent, and should not brown.

2. Sprinkle flour over onions, blend, and cook for 2 minutes.

3. Add boiling water gradually, stirring until soup thickens slightly. Add salt and pepper.

4. Simmer 20–30 minutes, or until serving time. Add bread 10 minutes before serving.

5. Immediately before serving, beat egg yolks with vinegar and stir gradually into the soup, mixing well.

Hearth Method:

1. Use a large hanging iron pot. Melt butter over heat. Swing pot toward hearth to add onions, stir to coat with butter, and return to fire.

2. When translucent, pull pot toward hearth, add flour, blend, and allow to cook, using the heat of the iron pot.

3. Add boiling water gradually, stirring until soup thickens slightly. Add salt and pepper. Push crane back over fire.

4. Follow Steps 4 and 5 in the Modern Method recipe.

Yield: 10 servings

Winter Vegetable Soup

"To every gallon of water allow, when cut down small, a quart of the following vegetables: Equal quantities of turnips, carrots, and potatoes, three onions, two heads of celery, and a bunch of sweet herbs. Fry them brown in a quarter pound of butter. Add the water with salt and pepper and boil it till reduced to three quarts, and serve with fried toasted bread."

—The Practice of Cookery, 1830

1 cup chopped onion

3 stalks celery

1 pound carrots, peeled and sliced

1 turnip, peeled and sliced

4 potatoes, chopped

4 ounces butter

2 quarts boiling water

1 teaspoon salt

½ teaspoon pepper

1 teaspoon sage

1 teaspoon marjoram

1 teaspoon parsley

1 teaspoon summer savory

Modern Method:

1. Peel and chop vegetables.
2. Melt butter and heat until bubbly.
3. Add vegetables and cook until slightly golden.
4. Add herbs and boiling water (more or less water, according to desired thickness).
5. Simmer 45 minutes. Correct seasoning. Garnish with croutons if desired.

Hearth Method:

1. Follow Steps 1 and 2 in the Modern Method recipe, using large hanging kettle.
2. Take kettle from crane and place over hot coals to sauté vegetables.
3. Add water and herbs and finish cooking by hanging kettle from crane.
4. Follow Step 5 in Modern Method recipe.

Yield: 8–10 servings

HERBS

HERBS

RECIPES USING HERBS

Drying Herbs

"Sweet Herbs. Those in cookery are parsley, rocambole [leek], winter savory, thyme, bay-leaf, basil, mint, borage, rosemary, marjoram &c. The relishing herbs are tarragon, garden-cress, chervil, burnet, and green mustard.

"All herbs should be gathered while in blossom. If left till they have gone to seed, the strength goes into the seed. Those who have a little patch of ground will do well to raise the most important herbs, and those who have not, will do well to get them in quantities from some friend in the country; for apothecaries make a very great profit upon them.

"All herbs should be carefully kept from the air. Herb tea to do any good, should be made very strong."

—*The American Frugal Housewife*, 1832

Modern Method:

1. Pick flowering herbs on a dry day, and pinch off flowers.
2. Dry herbs, using one of several methods:
a. To air-dry in a warm place, gather several stalks, tie with string, leaving a loop to hang on a nail or on a long cord extended between two nails.
b. To take advantage of the heat of the pilot light in a gas oven, arrange the herbs loosely on a cookie sheet and place in oven. Turn from time to time until dry.
c. Use a commercially available drying box, following manufacturer's directions.
3. Crush herbs when dry and store them in an airtight bottle or tin, with a label identifying the contents and date of preparation.

Hearth Method:

1. Pick flowering herbs on a dry day, and pinch off flowers.

2. Lay them in the Dutch oven, near the fire. Rearrange from time to time, until the herbs thoroughly dry and the leaves crumble between the fingers.

3. Crush and store in an airtight bottle or tin, with a label identifying the contents and date of preparation.

Herb Crusher

Herbs for Cooking

"Sage is very useful for all kinds of stuffing. When dried and rubbed into powder it should be kept tight from air.

"Summer-savory is excellent to season soup, broth and sausages.

"Sweet-marjoram is the best of all herbs for broth and stuffing. Few people know how to keep the flavor of it. It should be gathered while in bud or blossom and dried in a tin kitchen at a moderate distance from the fire. When dry, it should be immediately rubbed, sifted, and corked up in a bottle carefully.

"Powder of fine herbs for flavoring Soups and Sauces when fresh herbs cannot be obtained.—Take dried parsley two ounces; of lemon-thyme, summer-savory, sweet marjoram and basil, one ounce each; dried lemon-peel one ounce; these must be dried thoroughly, pounded fine, the powder mixed, sifted, and bottled. You can add celery seeds if you like."

—The American Frugal Housewife, 1832

½ cup dried parsley

2 tablespoons thyme

2 tablespoons summer savory

2 tablespoons basil

2 tablespoons dried lemon peel

2 tablespoons celery seeds, optional

Modern and Hearth Methods:

1. Measure ingredients into a bowl.
2. Rub through a sieve or between the hands until finely crushed and well blended.
3. Store in a jar with a tight-fitting lid.

Yield: approximately 1 cup

Flavored Vinegars

6 sprigs fresh basil, or 4–6 celery stalks with leaves, or dill, burnet, borage, lovage, tarragon, or rosemary

Quart jar with a lid

1 quart white vinegar

"Basil Vinegar. Sweet basil is in full perfection about the middle of August. Fill a wide-mouthed bottle with the fresh green leaves of basil (these give much finer and more flavor than the dried,) and cover them with vinegar, or wine and let them steep for ten days; if you wish a very strong essence, strain the liquor, put it on some fresh leaves, and let them steep fourteen days or more. This is a very agreeable addition to sauces, soups and to the mixture usually made for salads.

"The flavor of the other sweet and savory herbs, celery and burnet &c may be procured, and preserved in the same manner by infusing them in wine or vinegar."

—The Cook's Oracle, 1823

Modern and Hearth Methods:

1. Wash freshly picked basil or other herb of choice and dry off as much moisture as possible.
2. Place basil or herbs in jar, but do not crowd. Fill with vinegar.
3. Store in a cool, dark place for 10–14 days. Strain through a cheesecloth into a clean jar for storage, or repeat steps 1 and 2 using fresh herbs and the steeped vinegar. After 10 days more, strain and discard herbs before use.

Yield: 1 quart

Vinegar for Salads

"Take of tarragon, savory, chives, eschalots, three ounces each; a handful of the tops of mint and balm, all dry and pounded; put into a wide-mouthed bottle, with a gallon of best vinegar; cork it close, set it in the sun and in a fortnight strain off and squeeze the herbs; let it stand a day to settle, and then strain it through a filtering bag."

—*The Cook's Oracle*, 1823

3 sprigs fresh tarragon

3 sprigs fresh savory

3 tablespoons chives

½ cup sliced shallots

2 sprigs fresh mint

2 sprigs fresh lemon balm

Gallon jug of vinegar

Cheesecloth

4 quart jars or bottles

Modern and Hearth Methods:

1. Combine herbs.
2. Remove approximately 1 cup of vinegar from gallon jug and put in herbs. Add more vinegar to fill, if necessary. Replace cap.
3. Leave in a warm place for two weeks.
4. Remove herbs from vinegar by straining and pressing out as much vinegar as possible.
5. Let settle for 24 hours.
6. Strain into 1-quart jars or bottles for storage.

Yield: 4 quarts

Mustard

¼ cup powdered mustard

¼ teaspoon salt, or 1 teaspoon sugar

2–3 tablespoons hot water, or milk

"Mustard is best when freshly made. Mix by degrees, the best ground mustard and a little fine salt with warm water; rub these a long time till perfectly smooth. Mild mustard.—Mix as above, but use milk instead of water and sugar instead of salt."

—*The Good Housekeeper*, 1839

Modern and Hearth Methods:
Combine ingredients in a deep glass or ceramic dish. Blend until smooth with a spoon.

Yield: ¼ cup

Spice and Herb Box

Herb Teas for Indigestion

"Throughwort [boneset] *is excellent for dyspepsy and every disorder occasioned by indigestion. Succory is a very valuable herb. The tea, sweetened with molasses, is good for the piles. It is a gentle and healthy physic, a preventive of dyspepsy, humors, inflammation and all the evils resulting from a restricted state of the system. Elderblow* [elderberry] *tea has a similar effect. It is cool and soothing and peculiarly efficacious either for babes or grown people, when the digestive powers are out of order. Summer-savory relieves the cholic. Penny-royal* [mint] *and tansy are good for the same purpose."*

—*The American Frugal Housewife*, 1832

1–2 teaspoons crushed herbs

¾ cup boiling water

Sugar, molasses, or honey

Modern and Hearth Methods:

1. Pour water over crushed herbs. Steep for 5 minutes.
2. Strain brewed herb tea into a cup or mug. Sweeten to taste.

Yield: 1 serving

"Avoid the necessity of a physician, if you can, by careful attention to your diet. Eat what best agrees with your system, and resolutely abstain from what hurts you, however well you may like it."

—Lydia Maria Child,
The American Frugal Housewife (Boston, 1832)

A Cool Summer Tankard

Juice of 2 lemons

2 tablespoons sugar

1 cup water

1 cup white port or May wine

8–10 borage leaves

Borage blossoms for garnish

"Borage is cultivated in our gardens on account of the supposed cordial virtues of its flowers, but they have long lost their reputation. In Italy its young and tender leaves are in common use both as a pot-herb and a salad. In France its flowers, with those of Nasturtium are put into salads as an ornament. In England it is now nearly neglected, but the flowers and upper leaves are sometimes used as an ingredient in that summer beverage composed of wine, water, lemon juice, and sugar, called a cool tankard, to which they seem to give an additional coolness."

—Family Kitchen Gardener, 1847

Modern and Hearth Methods:

1. Squeeze lemons, extracting ½ cup juice.
2. Combine all ingredients in a pitcher and chill.

Yield: 1 pint beverage

PUDDINGS

A Note on Sugar

The recipes in *The American Frugal Housewife* were written for a time in which granulated white sugar was not in everyday use. Common, everyday family dishes were often made using brown sugar or molasses. While we do not know exactly what brown sugar looked like in the early nineteenth century, the refining process removed the liquid from the molasses, resulting in a more crystallized product than plain molasses. By combining ½ cup of sugar with 2 tablespoons of molasses for each cup of sugar called for in the recipe, we can come reasonably close to reproducing the flavor of brown sugar.

The use of maple sugar in the past, especially in cooking, is a subject for speculation, because recipes calling for maple products are practically nonexistent. We do know that farmers who tapped their trees reduced the sap to sugar, rather than storing it as syrup, which develops mold without refrigeration. This sugar was probably used in place of store-bought brown sugar in baking cakes and pies.

Indian Pudding

"Indian pudding is good baked. Scald a quart of milk (skimmed milk will do) and stir in seven table spoonfuls of sifted Indian meal, a tea-spoonful of salt, a teacupful of molasses, and a great spoonful of ginger, or sifted cinnamon. Baked three or four hours. If you want whey, you must be sure and pour in a little cold milk, after it is all mixed."

—The American Frugal Housewife, 1832

1 quart milk

7 tablespoons cornmeal

1 teaspoon salt

¾ cup molasses

1 tablespoon ginger or 1 tablespoon cinnamon

½ cup cold milk, optional

Modern Method:

1. Heat milk to boiling point. Add cornmeal and salt and stir well.

2. Add molasses and spices, stirring to blend.

3. Pour into buttered, 2-quart baking dish, and add cold milk, if desired.

4. Bake in 325°F oven for 2 hours. Serve warm.

Hearth Method:

1. Heat milk in a shallow pottery baking dish on a trivet over coals. Add cornmeal and salt and stir well.

2. Remove from heat. Add molasses and spices, stirring to blend.

3. Add ½ cup cold milk, if desired.

4. Bake 4–5 hours in the brick oven. (The long cooking period is necessary because the oven cools as time passes.) If a Dutch oven is used, bake 2–2½ hours. Add fresh coals two or three times. Serve warm.

Yield: 8 servings

Stewed Pears

1 small beetroot

2 cups water

6 pears

¼ cup sugar

Grated peel of ½ lemon

"Slice and stew a small beet root in a pint of water; take out the beet; pare, core and quarter your pears, and stew in the same water; sweeten to your taste, and add a little lemon-peel."

—*The Good Housekeeper,* 1839

Note: This recipe was developed as a result of the growing temperance movement of the nineteenth century with the beet juice substituted for red wine that would have been used earlier.

Modern Method:

1. Peel beetroot and simmer in 2 cups of water for 15 minutes.
2. Peel, quarter, and core pears.
3. Remove beetroot from water; simmer pears in water until tender. Remove from heat and add sugar and lemon peel.

Hearth Method:

1. Follow Step 1 in the Modern Method recipe, using a hanging pot over the fire.
2. Follow Steps 2 and 3 in the Modern Method recipe. Pears will soften in 30 to 45 minutes depending on ripeness.

Yield: 6 servings of four sections of pear

Red Currant or Pink Cream

"Squeeze three quarters of a pint of juice from red currants when full ripe, add to it rather more than a quarter of a pound of pounded loaf sugar, and the juice of one lemon: stir it into a pint and a half of cream, and whisk it till quite thick. Serve it in a glass dish, or in jelly glasses. It may be made with currant jelly, which mix with the lemon juice and sugar.

"Raspberry and strawberry cream may be made in the same way."

—*The Good Housekeeper,* 1839

2 cups red currants (or 1 cup red currant jelly and omit sugar)

1 lemon (2–3 tablespoons juice when squeezed)

²/₃ cup sugar

2 cups cream

Modern and Hearth Methods:

1. Squeeze approximately 1 cup of juice from fresh or thawed frozen red currants using a cloth jelly bag. Cut lemon in half and squeeze out juice. Combine currant juice, lemon juice, and sugar or combine current jelly and lemon juice (omit sugar). (If using prepared jelly, mix with lemon juice until liquefied.)
2. Whip cream until stiff peaks form and fold in prepared juices. Serve in a glass dish or in individual wine glasses. Garnish with a twist of lemon rind, if desired.

Yield: 3½ cups

Quince Cheese

4–5 medium quinces

1½ pounds brown sugar

"Have fine ripe quinces, and pare and core them. Cut them into pieces and weigh them; and to each pound of the cut quinces, allow half a pound of the best brown sugar. Put the cores and parings into a kettle with water enough to cover them, keeping the lid of the kettle closed. When you find they are all boiled to pieces and quite soft, strain off the water over the sugar, and when it is entirely dissolved, put it over the fire and boil it to a thick syrup, skimming it well. When no more scum rises, put in the quinces, cover them closely, and boil them all day over a slow fire, stirring them and mashing them down with a spoon till they are a thick smooth paste. Then take it out, and put it into buttered tin pans or deep dishes. Let it set to get cold. It will then turn out so firm that you may cut it into slices like cheese. Keep it in a dry place in broad stone pots. It is intended for the tea table."

—*Directions for Cookery*, 1851

Note: The term *cheese* used to describe this translucent red and intensely sweet accompaniment to the tea table or dessert buffet refers to the long-cooking and pressing technique used in the preparation of the dish. *Cheese* is also the term used for the layers of apple pulp and straw that are pressed together for cider-making, as well as the boiled, chopped, and pressed meat from a pig's head (head cheese).

Modern Method:

1. Peel and core quinces. Place peels and cores in pot and cover with water. Boil for 1 hour, replacing water if necessary.

2. While peels and cores are boiling, cut fruit into ¼-inch dice. Strain water from peels and cores, reserving liquid. Discard peels and cores. Cover diced quince with reserved liquid and boil in pot for 1 hour or until tender.

3. Add brown sugar to boiled quince and simmer 45 minutes. The mixture will become very thick and red. Pour into greased square baking pan or pie plate and chill until set, weighing down gently with a plate.

Hearth Method:

Follow Steps 1–3 in Modern Method recipe, boiling in a tin-lined kettle hanging from a crane over the fire.

Yield: 12 slices

Quince Cream with Ginger

6 quinces

2-inch piece of fresh ginger root

2 cups cream

½ cup sugar

¼ teaspoon rosewater

"Take four or five ripe quinces, and roast them, but not to soften them; pare, core, slice them thin, and then boil them slowly in a pint of good cream with a little ginger; when tolerably thick, strain it, add sugar to your taste and flavor it with rose-water."

—The Cook's Own Book, 1832

Modern Method:

1. Steam unpeeled whole quinces in the top of a double boiler until tender enough to cut. Peel and core each fruit. Peel ginger root and cut into thin slices.
2. Combine cream and fruit in the top of a double boiler and cook until it thickens and fruit is very soft.
3. Push through a strainer or sieve. Virtually everything should be used; only a very small amount of fiber will be discarded.
4. Add the sugar and rosewater.
5. Serve chilled in a glass bowl or in individual wine glasses.

Hearth Method:

1. Roast unpeeled whole quinces on a spit until browned and soft. Preheat a red-ware bowl on a trivet over coals.
2. Remove the softened fruit from the heat. Peel and core each fruit. Peel ginger root and cut into thin slices.
3. Combine cream and fruit in the heated redware bowl and cook until it thickens and fruit is very soft, changing coals beneath trivet as necessary. It will cook slowly, taking approximately 1 hour to thicken.
4. Follow Steps 3–5 in the Modern Method recipe.

Yield: 8 ½-cup servings

Lemon Pudding

"Boil in water, in a closely covered sauce-pan, two large lemons till quite tender; take out the seeds and pound the lemons to a paste; add a quarter of a pound of pounded loaf sugar, the same of fresh butter beaten to a cream, and three well beaten eggs; mix all together and bake it in a tin lined with puff pastry; take it out, strew over the top grated loaf sugar."

—*The Good Housekeeper*, 1839

2 lemons

½ cup plus 2 tablespoons white sugar

8 tablespoons butter

3 eggs

½ recipe for Puff Pastry for Filled Turnovers (recipe on page 150)

Modern Method:

1. Prepare puff pastry.

2. In medium saucepan, cover lemons with water. Bring to a boil and reduce heat. Simmer in covered pan until very tender, approximately 25 minutes. Check to water to maintain level.

3. When tender, remove lemons from water and cut in half to remove seeds.

4. Puree lemons in food processor or blender until smooth.

5. Add ½ cup sugar, butter, and eggs to the mixture and blend.

6. Pour into a pie plate that has been lined with the pastry.

7. Bake for 45 minutes or until set in a 350°F oven. Sprinkle with remaining sugar when removed from the oven. Cool before serving.

Hearth Method:

1. Prepare Puff Pastry

2. Follow Steps 2 and 3 in the Modern Method, using medium hanging kettle.

3. Using masher and wooden bowl, puree lemons until they are smooth.

4. Follow Steps 5 and 6 in the Modern Method.

5. Bake for 45 minutes in a preheated brick oven or preheated Dutch oven with coals above and beneath. Sprinkle with remaining sugar when removed from the oven. Cool before serving.

Yield: one 9-inch pie

Crookneck or Winter Squash Pudding

3 cups peeled and sliced butternut squash

3 apples, peeled, cored, and finely chopped

3 eggs

1 cup cream

¾ cup sugar

2 tablespoon white port wine

1 tablespoon rosewater, optional

1 teaspoon grated nutmeg

Dash of salt

1 tablespoon flour

¼ cup unflavored bread crumbs

"Core, boil and skin a good squash and bruise it well; take 6 large apples, pared, cored and stewed tender, mix together; add 6 or 7 spoonfuls of dry bread crumbs or biscuit rendered fine as meal, one pint milk or cream, 2 spoons of rose-water, 2 do. Wine, 5 or 6 egg beaten and strained, nutmeg, salt and sugar to your taste, one spoon flour, beat all smartly together, bake one hour."

—American Cookery, 1796

Note: In the early nineteenth century, the term *crookneck* was used to refer to any squash with a long bent or crooked neck. The most common winter squash grown during the time was the Canada Crookneck, which resembles the modern butternut in color, flavor, and size.

Modern Method:
1. Boil squash in covered saucepan with a small amount of water until soft. Drain water and mash squash. (Alternatively, squash may be cooked in microwave.)
2. Boil apples in covered saucepan with a small amount of water until soft (or cook in microwave). Mash apples and add to squash.
3. Beat eggs and cream. Add sugar, wine, rosewater (optional), nutmeg, salt, flour, and bread crumbs, and stir well.
4. Combine mixture with squash and apples. Pour into a 9-inch buttered baking dish.
5. Bake in pre-heated 350°F oven for 1 hour.

Hearth Method:

1. Follow Step 1 in the Modern Method, using a hanging kettle.

2. Simmer apples with a little water in a redware bowl on a trivet over a pile of hot coals until tender. Mash apples and add to squash.

3. Follow Steps 3 and 4.

4. Bake in bake oven that has been preheated for 1 hour or from which breads and cakes have been removed. Bake 1 hour or until set. If using Dutch oven, preheat for 10 minutes and bake with coals on top of the lid and beneath the Dutch oven for 1 hour, changing the coals after 30 minutes.

Yield: 8 servings

Custard Pudding

4 cups milk

1 stick cinnamon, optional

5 eggs

½ cup brown sugar

¼ teaspoon nutmeg or cinnamon

¼ teaspoon salt

"Custard puddings sufficiently good for common use can be made with five eggs to a quart of milk, sweetened with brown sugar, and spiced with cinnamon, or nutmeg, and very little salt. It is well to boil your milk, and set it away till it gets cold. Boiling milk enriches it so much that boiled skim-milk is about as good as new milk. A little cinnamon, or lemon peel, or peach leaves, if you do not dislike the taste, boiled in the milk, and afterwards strained from it, give a pleasant flavor. Bake fifteen or twenty minutes."

—*The American Frugal Housewife*, 1832

Modern Method:

1. Scald milk with cinnamon stick and set aside until cool. When ready to proceed, remove cinnamon stick.
2. Beat eggs, add brown sugar, spices, salt, and cooled milk.
3. Pour into 2-quart baking dish. For best results, place baking dish in a pan of hot water in the oven. Bake in 325°F oven for 1 hour, or until knife inserted near the middle comes out clean. It will continue cooking and become more firm as it cools. Serve cold.

Hearth Method:

1. In a shallow pan, scald milk and cinnamon stick on a trivet over coals. Set aside to cool. When ready to proceed, remove cinnamon stick.
2. Beat eggs with a fork or whisk. Add sugar, spices, salt, and cooled milk.
3. Pour into 2-quart baking dish. To bake, use a brick oven that has been preheated for 1 hour, or put custard in after other items, such as breads or cakes, have baked. Bake pudding 1 hour. If using a Dutch oven, do not preheat. Put coals on lid and underneath. Bake 45 minutes or until custard is set. It will continue cooking and become more firm as it cools. Serve cold.

Yield: 8 servings

Bird's Nest Pudding

"If you wish to make what is called 'Bird's nest puddings,' prepare your custard,—take eight or ten pleasant apples, pare them and dig out the core, but leave them whole, set them in a pudding dish, pour your custard over them, and bake them about thirty minutes."

—The American Frugal Housewife, 1832

½ recipe for Custard Pudding

6 apples

Modern Method:

1. Follow Steps 1 and 2 in the recipe on page 122.
2. Core the apples. Do not peel them. Place close together in a 9-inch baking dish or 9-inch pottery pie plate. Pour custard over apples.
3. Bake in 325°F oven for 45 minutes or until set.

Hearth Method:

1. Follow Steps 1 and 2 in the recipe on page 122.
2. Follow Step 2 in the Modern Method recipe.
3. Bake in oven that has preheated for 1 hour or from which breads and cakes have already been removed. Bake 2 hours. If using a Dutch oven, do not preheat. Place coals beneath and on the lid. Bake 30–45 minutes or until custard is set.

Yield: 6 servings

Cheap Custard

4 cups milk

½ stick cinnamon, optional

3 tablespoons rice flour,
cornstarch, or cooked rice

⅓–½ cup sugar

1 egg

"One quart of milk, boiled; when boiling, add three table spoonfuls of ground rice or rice that is boiled, mixed smooth and fine in cold milk, and one egg beaten; give it one boil up and sweeten to your taste; peach leaves or any spice you please, boiled in the milk."

—The American Frugal Housewife, 1832

Modern Method:

1. Heat 3½ cups of milk to the boiling point, with cinnamon stick, if desired.
2. In a large bowl, blend remaining milk with rice or cornstarch and sugar, and add beaten egg.
3. Remove cinnamon stick from milk and add 1 cup of hot milk to the mixture in the bowl. Blend and pour mixture into pan containing the remainder of the milk.
4. Heat slowly, stirring often, until slightly thickened. It will not be firm.
5. Serve warm or cold as a sauce over fruit or puddings, or in a trifle.

Hearth Method:

1. Follow Step 1 in the Modern Method recipe, using a hanging pot over a moderate to hot fire.
2. Follow Steps 2 and 3 in the Modern Method recipe.
3. Heat slowly over moderate to slow fire, stirring often, until slightly thickened.
4. Follow Step 5 in the Modern Method recipe.

Yield: 4 cups

Rice Pudding

"If you have some rice left cold, break it up in a little warm milk, pour custard over it, and bake it as long as you should custard. It makes very good puddings and pies."

— *The American Frugal Housewife*, 1832

½ cup warm milk

1 cup cooked rice

½ recipe for Custard Pudding

Modern Method:

1. Combine milk and rice over heat. Break up rice with a fork, and heat gently until milk is absorbed.

2. Follow Steps 1 and 2 of the recipe on page 122.

3. Place rice in baking dish and cover with custard. Bake in 325°F oven for 30–40 minutes.

Hearth Method:

1. Combine milk and rice in baking dish set on a trivet over coals. Break up rice with a fork and heat gently until milk is absorbed.

2. Follow Steps 1 and 2 of the recipe on page 122.

3. Pour custard over rice. Set baking dish in a Dutch oven that has not been preheated. Place coals above and below and bake about 45 minutes.

Yield: 6 servings

Rice Pudding with Fruit

¾ cup uncooked rice (not quick-cooking)

3 cups milk

1 egg

1 cup fresh or dried fruit: currants, gooseberries, apples pared and quartered, or raisins

⅓ cup brown sugar, less if dried fruits are used

2 tablespoons brown sugar

1 teaspoon nutmeg

"Swell the rice with a very little milk over the fire; then mix fruit of any kind with it—currants, gooseberries scalded, pared and quartered apples; put one egg in to bind the rice; boil it well, and serve it with sugar, beat together, with nutmeg, or mace."

—*The New England Economical Housekeeper*, 1845

Modern Method:

1. Put rice and milk in a saucepan. Cover and simmer slowly until rice is soft and liquid is absorbed, about 15–20 minutes.

2. Stir in beaten egg, fruit, and brown sugar and cook for 5 minutes or until thickened.

3. Combine remaining sugar and nutmeg. Serve pudding warm with nutmeg sugar.

Hearth Method:

1. Cook rice in milk in a hanging pot over a slow fire until rice is soft and liquid is absorbed, about 45 minutes.

2. Add beaten egg, fruit, and brown sugar and cook 5–10 minutes or until thickened.

3. Combine remaining sugar and nutmeg. Serve pudding warm with nutmeg sugar.

Yield: 6 servings

Quaking Plum Pudding

"Take slices of light bread and spread them thin with butter, and lay in the pudding dish layers of bread and raisins, within an inch of the top; then take five eggs and beat them well, and mix them with a quart of milk, and pour it over the pudding; add salt and spice to suit your taste; you may put in a cup of sugar, and eat it with butter, or you may omit the sugar, and serve it up with sweet sauce. Bake it twenty or twenty-five minutes. Before you use the raisins, boil them in a very little water, and put it all in."

—*The New England Economical Housekeeper*, 1845

1 cup raisins

½ cup water or brandy

½ loaf bread with a firm crust

¼–½ cup butter

5 eggs

4 cups milk

½ teaspoon salt

1 teaspoon cinnamon

¼ teaspoon freshly grated nutmeg

Modern Method:

1. Cook raisins in water or brandy for 15 minutes.
2. Slice bread, butter slices, line a 2-quart baking dish with a layer of slices.
3. Sprinkle with raisins. Continue to build layers until all bread and raisins are used.
4. Beat eggs, add milk and remaining ingredients. Pour over bread.
5. Bake 1 hour in 350°F oven.

Hearth Method:

1. Cook raisins and water or brandy in a small pan on a trivet over coals near the fire for 15–20 minutes or until raisins are plump.
2. Follow Steps 2–4 in the Modern Method recipe.
3. Bake in a preheated Dutch oven up to an hour. Cooking time will vary depending on the shape and thickness of the baking dish. If it is cooking very slowly after 45 minutes, change the coals above and beneath the Dutch oven.

Yield: 8 servings

Hasty Pudding

1 cup sifted cornmeal

4¼ cups water

½ teaspoon salt

Molasses or maple syrup

Milk

Butter

Brown sugar

"Boil water, a quart, three pints, or two quarts, according to the size of your family; sift your meal, stir five or six spoonfuls of it thoroughly into a bowl of water; when the water in the kettle boils, pour into it the contents of the bowl; stir it well, and let it boil up thick; put in salt to suit your own taste, then stand over the kettle, and sprinkle in meal, handful after handful, stirring it very thoroughly all the time, and letting it boil between whiles. When it is so thick that you stir it with great difficulty, it is about right. It takes about half an hour's cooking. Eat it with milk or molasses. Either Indian meal or rye meal may be used. If the system is in a restricted state, nothing can be better than rye hasty pudding and West India molasses. This diet would save many a one the horrors of dyspepsia."

—*The American Frugal Housewife*, 1832

Modern Method:

1. Stir 3 tablespoons cornmeal into ¼ cup water.
2. Boil remaining water, stir in cornmeal and water mixture. Let mixture come to a boil. Add salt.
3. Stirring constantly, add remaining cornmeal ¼ cup at a time, letting pudding come to a boil between additions.
4. Serve pudding hot with molasses and milk; when cold, cut leftovers into slices and fry in butter or lard. Serve for breakfast with butter and brown sugar or molasses.

Hearth Method:

1. Follow Step 1 in the Modern Method recipe.
2. Boil remaining water in a small hanging pot. Pull crane and pot from high heat. Stir in cornmeal and water mixture. Return to fire and bring to a boil. Add salt.
3. Pull crane and pot toward hearth. Add remaining cornmeal ¼ cup at a time, stirring to blend and returning to fire until mixture boils after each addition. This will take about ½ hour.

4. Serve pudding hot with molasses and milk.

5. When cold, cut leftovers into slices to fry in butter or lard. Melt butter in a hanging griddle over moderate fire. Pull away from heat to put slices into pan and then return to heat, until browned and ready to be turned. Serve for breakfast with butter and brown sugar or molasses.

Yield: 10–12 servings

"There was always a Fast Day, which I am afraid most of us younger ones regarded merely as a day when we were to eat unlimited quantities of molasses-gingerbread instead of sitting down to our regular meals."

—Lucy Larcom,
A New England Girlhood (Boston, 1889)

A George Pudding

FILLING:

1 lemon

⅓ cup uncooked rice (not quick-cooking)

1 cup milk

6 baking apples

¼ cup white wine

3 eggs

½ cup citron or preserved orange peel, optional

½ cup sugar

CRUST:

¼ cup butter

1 cup flour

1 egg

3 tablespoons water

SAUCE:

½ cup sherry, Madeira, or apple cider

1 tablespoon brown sugar

2 egg yolks

1 tablespoon butter

"Boil very tender a handful of whole rice in a small quantity of milk with a large piece of lemonpeel. Let it drain; then mix with it a dozen of good sized apples, boiled to a pulp, and as dry as possible. Add a glass of white wine, the yolks of five eggs, and two ounces of orange and citron cut thin; make it pretty sweet. Line a mould or basin with a very good paste: beat the five whites of the eggs to a very strong froth and mix with the other ingredients: fill the mould, and bake it of a fine brown color. Serve it with the bottom upward, with the following sauce: two glasses of wine, a spoonful of sugar, the yolk of two eggs, and a bit of butter as large as a walnut: simmer without boiling, and pour to and from the saucepan, till of a proper thickness, and put in the dish."

—*A New System of Domestic Cookery*, 1807

Modern Method:

1. Cut lemon into thin slices and remove seeds. Combine rice, lemon slices, and milk in a saucepan. Cook covered over low heat for 45 minutes, or until rice is soft and milk is absorbed.

2. Make crust to line 9-inch pie plate or 1¾-quart ovenproof bowl. Cut butter into flour, and add egg beaten with water. Roll out piecrust and line the dish.

3. Peel, core, and chop apples.

4. When rice is cooked, mix the apples and remaining ingredients with the rice, and spoon into prepared dish.

5. Bake 1 hour at 375°F.

6. Just before serving, combine the wine or cider, brown sugar, beaten egg yolks, and butter in a small saucepan over low heat. Simmer until blended and thickened.

7. Invert cooled pudding onto serving plate and top with sauce.

Hearth Method:

1. Cut lemon into thin slices and remove seeds. Combine rice, lemon slices, and milk in a small hanging pot. Cook over a slow fire or close to the crane if fire is hot, so that milk does not curdle. Cook until rice is soft and milk is absorbed.

2. Follow Steps 2–4 in the Modern Method recipe.

3. Bake in preheated Dutch oven for 1 hour; 1½ hours in moderate bake-oven.

4. Follow Step 6 in the Modern Method recipe, using a small pan on a trivet over coals.

5. Follow Step 7 in the Modern Method recipe.

Yield: 8 servings

Common Sweet Sauce

2 cups boiling water

2 tablespoons flour

2 tablespoons molasses or sugar

1 tablespoon butter

1 tablespoon rosewater

¼ cup wine, optional

¼ teaspoon nutmeg

"One sauce answers for common use for all sorts of pudding. Flour-and-water stirred into boiling water, sweetened to your taste with either molasses or sugar, according to your ideas of economy; a great spoonful of rosewater if you have it; butter half as big as a hen's egg. If you want to make it very nice, put in a glass of wine, and grate nutmeg over the top."

—*The American Frugal Housewife,* 1832

Modern Method:

1. Boil water in saucepan. Remove 2 tablespoons of water and add to flour to make a thick paste.

2. Stir flour and water paste into water in saucepan. Continue stirring until it thickens, and cook over low heat for 10 minutes.

3. Remove from heat. Add molasses or sugar, butter, rosewater, and wine, if desired. Stir to blend. Sprinkle nutmeg over before serving. Serve hot.

Hearth Method:

1. Follow Step 1 in the Modern Method recipe, using a tin pan.

2. Stir remaining water into paste, heating pan on a trivet over coals. Continue stirring until mixture thickens, and cook for 15–20 minutes.

3. Follow Step 3 in the Modern Method recipe.

Yield: 2 cups

Better Sweet Sauce

"When you wish a better sauce than common, take a quarter of a pound of butter and the same of sugar, mould them well together with your hand, add a little wine, if you choose. Make it into a lump, set it away to cool, and grate nutmeg over it."

—The American Frugal Housewife, 1832

¼ pound butter

½ cup sugar

1 tablespoon wine or brandy

¼ teaspoon nutmeg

Modern and Hearth Methods:

1. Cream butter and sugar.
2. Stir in wine or brandy, and mold into a ball. Chill for two hours or more.
3. Sprinkle grated nutmeg over hard sauce before serving over warm pudding.

Yield: ¾ cup

"May a millennium of Virtue, Peace and happiness, soon bless the whole family of man."

—Abner Gay,
Account Book, 1815, Old Sturbridge Village Research Library

COMMON PIES

Piecrust

"To make pie crust for common use, a quarter of a pound of butter is enough for a half a pound of flour. Take out about a quarter part of the flour you intend to use, and lay it aside. Into the remainder of the flour rub butter thoroughly with your hands, until it is so short that a handful of it, clasped tight, will remain in a ball, without any tendency to fall in pieces. Then wet it with cold water, roll it out on a board, rub over the surface with flour, stick little lumps of butter all over it, sprinkle some flour over the butter, and roll the dough all up; flour the paste, and flour the rolling-pin; roll it lightly and quickly; flour it again; stick in bits of butter; do it up; flour the rolling-pin, and roll it quickly and lightly; and so on, till you have used up your butter. Always roll from you. Pie crust should be made as cold as possible, and set in a cool place; but be careful it does not freeze. Do not use more flour than you can help in sprinkling and rolling. The paste should not be rolled out more than three times; or it will not be flaky."

—*The American Frugal Housewife,* 1832

2 cups sifted flour, measured after sifting

½ cup butter

6 tablespoons cold water

Modern and Hearth Methods:

1. Measure and set aside ½ cup flour and 2 tablespoons butter.
2. Rub the remaining butter into the flour using your hand as the tool.
3. Gently stir in cold water until it starts to form a ball.
4. Roll dough out on well-floured board with a floured rolling pin, dot with 1 tablespoon reserved butter, and sprinkle 1 tablespoon reserved flour. Roll up the dough like a jelly roll. Flour lightly and roll to a ¼-inch thickness.
5. Repeat Step 4 twice, to use all butter and flour.
6. Store in a cool place until needed.

Yield: two 9-inch piecrusts

Mince Pies

1¼ pounds beef round or leftover roast

¼ pound suet

1½ pounds apples

1 cup raisins or currants

½ cup white sugar

½ cup brown sugar

⅛ teaspoon pepper

½ teaspoon salt

2 teaspoons cinnamon

1 teaspoon clove

2 teaspoons nutmeg

¼ cup brandy

2 cups cider or apple juice

Double recipe Piecrust (recipe on page 135)

1 tablespoon butter

"Boil a tender, nice piece of beef—any piece that is clear from sinews and gristle; boil it till it is perfectly tender. When it is cold, chop it very fine, and be very careful to get out every particle of bone and gristle. The suet is sweeter and better to boil half an hour or more in the liquor the beef has been boiled in; but few people do this. Pare, core, and chop the apples fine. If you use raisins, stone them. If you use currants, wash and dry them at the fire. Two pounds of beef, after it is chopped; three quarters of a pound of suet; one pound and a quarter of sugar; three pounds of apples; two pounds of currants, or raisins. Put in a gill of brandy; lemon-brandy is better, if you have any prepared. Make it quite moist with new cider. I should not think a quart would be too much; the more moist the better, if it does not spill out into the oven. A very little pepper. If you use corn meat, or tongue, for pies, it should be well soaked, and boiled very tender. If you use fresh beef, salt is necessary in the seasoning. One ounce of cinnamon, one ounce of cloves. Two nutmegs add to the pleasantness of the flavor; and a bit of sweet butter put upon the top of each pie, makes them rich; but these are not necessary. Baked three quarters of an hour. If your apples are rather sweet, grate in a whole lemon."

—*The American Frugal Housewife*, 1832

Modern Method:

1. If uncooked meat is used, simmer beef 2–3 hours or until very tender, adding suet for last ½ hour of cooking.
2. When cooked, chop beef and suet very fine, into about ¼-inch pieces.
3. Pare, core, and chop apples to make 3 cups.
4. Mix beef, suet, apples, raisins or currants, white and brown sugars, spices, brandy, and cider or apple juice.

5. Prepare piecrust.

6. Line pie plates with pastry, fill each with half of meat mixture. Cover with top crusts, seal edges, slit holes on top for steam to escape. If desired, spread a thick layer of butter on pastry for flaky upper crust.

7. Bake ¾ hour in 400°–425°F oven.

Hearth Method:

1. In a hanging kettle, simmer beef for 2 hours, adding suet for last ½ hour of cooking.

2. Following Steps 2–6 in the Modern Method recipe.

3. Set pies in metal pie plates on trivets. If pottery pie plates are used, set pies directly on floor of very hot bake-oven. Or use a preheated Dutch oven with coals on lid and beneath. Change coals after 25 minutes to maintain a high temperature. Bake 45 minutes.

Yield: two 9-inch pies

Pumpkin or Squash Pie

Small pumpkin or squash, or use Pumpkin Leather (recipe on page 204)

½ recipe Piecrust (recipe on page 135)

2 eggs, or 1 or 2 more "to make your pie richer"

2 cups milk (if you add eggs, reduce milk by ¼–½ cup)

½ cup molasses

Dash of salt

2 tablespoons cinnamon

1 tablespoon ginger

Peel of ½ lemon, grated

"For common family pumpkin pies, three eggs do very well to a quart of milk. Stew your pumpkin, and strain it through a sieve, or colander. Take out the seeds and pare the pumpkin, or squash, before you stew it; but do not scrape the inside; the part nearest the seed is the sweetest part of the squash. Stir in the stewed pumpkin, till it is as thick as you can stir it round rapidly and easily. If you want to make your pie richer, make it thinner, and add another egg. One egg to a quart of milk makes very decent pies. Sweeten it to your taste, with molasses or sugar; some pumpkins require more sweetening than others. Two tea-spoonfuls of salt; two great spoonfuls of sifted cinnamon; one great spoonful of ginger. Ginger will answer very well alone for spice, if you use enough of it. The outside of a lemon grated in is nice. The more eggs, the better the pie; some put an egg to a gill of milk. This should bake from forty to fifty minutes, and even ten minutes longer, if very deep."

—*The American Frugal Housewife*, 1832

Modern Method:

1. Cut up the pumpkin or squash, remove seeds, and pare the outside rind. Simmer in a covered saucepan in a small amount of water until tender. Drain water and discard.
2. While pumpkin or squash cooks, prepare piecrust.
3. Force pumpkin through a sieve or use a food mill. Measure 2 cups puree for each pie. Remainder may be frozen or dried for future use.
4. Beat eggs and add milk. When blended, add pumpkin, molasses, salt, cinnamon, ginger, and lemon, and stir well.
5. Pour into 9-inch pie plate. Bake in 400°F oven for 15 minutes, then turn down to 375°F for 30 minutes or until set. Cool before serving.

Hearth Method:

1. Cut up pumpkin, remove seeds, and pare the outside rind. Simmer, covered with water, in a hanging kettle over a moderate fire until tender. Take out pumpkin and discard cooking water.

2. While pumpkin or squash cooks, prepare piecrust.

3. Follow Steps 3 and 4 in the Modern Method recipe.

4. Pour into pie shell in a 9-inch pottery pie plate. Bake 50–60 minutes in a hot brick oven. Or place the pie plate on a trivet and bake 50–60 minutes in a pre-heated Dutch oven with coals on lid and beneath. Coals will not have to be changed.

Yield: one 9-inch pie

Cranberry Pie

½ recipe Piecrust (recipe on page 135)

1 pound whole cranberries

2–3 cups sugar

2 cups water

¼ teaspoon nutmeg or cinnamon

"Cranberry pies need very little spice. A little nutmeg, or cinnamon, improves them. They need a great deal of sweetening. It is well to stew the sweetening with them; at least a part of it. It is easy to add, if you find them too sour for your taste. When cranberries are strained, and added to about their own weight in sugar, they make very delicious tarts. No upper crust."

—*The American Frugal Housewife*, 1832

Modern Method:

1. Prepare piecrust.
2. Place piecrust in a 9-inch pie plate or as 12–16 individual tarts. Bake for 20 minutes.
3. While crust bakes, combine cranberries, 2 cups sugar, and 2 cups water in saucepan. Simmer until cranberries pop and syrup has thickened. Add spice. Taste, and add sugar if the mixture seems too tart.
4. Spoon into the piecrust or tarts. Bake in 350°F oven for 30 minutes.

Hearth Method:

1. Prepare piecrust.
2. Bake for 20 minutes in a preheated Dutch oven. (Tin tart pans will not work in brick oven; use cast iron or a 9-inch pottery pie plate.)
3. Follow Step 3 in the Modern Method recipe, using a hanging kettle or skillet over a moderate fire.
4. Spoon mixture into the piecrust or tarts.
5. Bake in a moderate brick oven or preheated Dutch oven for 30 minutes.

Yield: one 9-inch pie or 12–16 tarts

Orange Pudding

"Grate the yellow rind of the orange and the lime, and squeeze the juice into a saucer or soup-plate, taking out all the seeds. Stir the butter and sugar to a cream. Beat the eggs as light as possible, and then stir them by degrees into the butter and sugar. Add, gradually, the liquor and rose-water, and then by degrees, the orange and lime. Stir all well together.

"Have ready a sheet of puff-paste, made of five ounces of sifted flour, and a quarter of a pound of fresh butter. Lay the paste in a buttered soup-plate. Trim and notch the edges, and then put in the mixture. Bake it about half an hour, in a moderate oven. Grate loaf sugar over it, before you send it to the table."

—*Seventy Five Receipts,* 1828

½ recipe for Puff Pastry (page 150)

2 oranges

1 lime

4 ounces butter

½ cup sugar

3 eggs

¼ cup white port wine

¼ cup brandy

1 teaspoon rosewater

Modern Method:

1. Prepare puff pastry recipe. Line 8-inch pie plate with pastry.
2. Grate rind from orange and lime. Cut in half and juice, removing seeds.
3. Cream together butter and sugar. Beat eggs until light, then gradually add to butter and sugar mixture.
4. Add liquor, rosewater, and reserved juice and rind to the mixture, then pour into prepared pastry crust.
5. Bake in a preheated 375°F oven for 35-40 minutes or until a knife inserted in the center comes out clean. Cool before serving. Sprinkle with white sugar.

Hearth Method:

1. Follow Steps 1–4 in Modern Method.
2. Bake 35–40 minutes in preheated Dutch oven with hot coals on lid and below, or 40 minutes in moderate bake oven.

Yield: one 8-inch pie

Carrot Pie

1½ pounds carrots

½ recipe Piecrust (recipe on page 135)

3 eggs

2 cups milk

½ teaspoon salt

2 teaspoons cinnamon

1 teaspoon ginger

Grated rind of ½ lemon

½ cup molasses

"Carrot pies are made like squash pies. The carrots should be boiled very tender, skinned and sifted. Both carrot pies and squash pies should be baked without an upper crust, in deep plates. To be baked an hour, in quite a hot oven."

—The American Frugal Housewife, 1832

Modern Method:

1. Cook carrots, peel, and mash or puree.
2. While carrots cook, prepare piecrust.
3. Mix together 1½–2 cups pureed carrots, beaten eggs, milk, salt, cinnamon, ginger, lemon rind, and molasses.
4. Pour into piecrust.
5. Bake 1 hour in 350°F oven.

Hearth Method:

1. Follow Step 1 in the Modern Method recipe, using a hanging pot over a moderate fire.
2. Follow Steps 2–4 in the Modern Method recipe.
3. Bake pie on a trivet in moderate brick oven for 50–60 minutes, or bake in preheated Dutch oven with coals on lid and beneath for 50–60 minutes.

Yield: one 9-inch pie

Dried Apple and Cranberry Pie

"Take two quarts dried apples, put them into an earthen pot that contains one gallon, fill it with water and set it in a hot oven, adding one handful of cranberries; after baking one hour fill the pot again with water; when done and the apple cold, strain it and add thereto the juice of three or four limes, raisins, sugar, orange peel and cinnamon to your taste."

—*American Cookery,* 1814

2 cups dried apples

Water to cover apples

2 cups cranberries

¾ cup brown sugar (packed)

½ cup raisins

1 teaspoon cinnamon

1 tablespoon orange peel

2 limes

Piecrust for double-crust pie (recipe on page 135)

Modern Method:

1. Cover dried apples with water. Soak 2–3 hours. Drain water, reserving 1 cup.
2. In saucepan, simmer soaked apples, 1 cup water, and cranberries until cranberries start to burst.
3. Remove from heat, add sugar, raisins, cinnamon, orange peel, and the juice of two limes.
4. Prepare piecrust. Pour mixture into pie plate lined with lower crust. Cover with top crust.
5. Bake in preheated 400°F oven 1 hour.

Hearth Method:

1. Follow Step 1 in the Modern Method recipe.
2. Warm a large redware bowl near fire. When bowl is warm add apples, 1 cup water, and cranberries and simmer on a trivet over hot coals until cranberries start to burst. (*Note:* Make sure redware bowl is warmed near fire before being placed over hot coals. Cold redware will crack very easily!)
3. Follow Steps 3 and 4 in the Modern Method recipe.
4. Bake for 1 hour in a preheated bake-oven or use a bake-kettle and lid that have been preheated 15 minutes. If using the bake-kettle, change coals after 25 minutes of baking.

Yield: one 9-inch pie

Apple Pie

6 cups apples, fresh or dried, or 2 cups applesauce (recipe on page 197)

½ cup brown sugar

½ teaspoon cloves or cinnamon

Piecrust for double-crust pie (recipe on page 135)

1 tablespoon butter

½ teaspoon salt, optional

1 tablespoon lemon peel, if apples are sweet

1 tablespoon lemon brandy or rosewater, optional

"When you make apple pies, stew your apples very little indeed; just strike them through, to make them tender. Some people do not stew them at all, but cut them up in very thin slices, and lay them in the crust. Pies made in this way may retain more of the spirit of the apple; but I do not think the seasoning mixes in as well. Put in sugar to your taste; it is impossible to make a precise rule, because apples vary so much in acidity. A very little salt, and a small piece of butter in each pie, makes them richer. Cloves and cinnamon are both suitable spice. Lemon-brandy and rose-water are both excellent. A wine-glass full of each is sufficient for three or four pies. If your apples lack spirit, grate in a whole lemon."

—The American Frugal Housewife, 1832

Modern Method:

1. To prepare apples, follow one of these three methods:

a. Peel and slice apples, toss with sugar and spice until all are coated.

b. Peel and core whole apples, slice into rings. Put into saucepan with 1 inch of water on the bottom, sugar, and spices. Stew for 10 minutes.

c. Put dried apples in a bowl and cover with water. They will swell up in a couple of hours in a warm place. Put apples, a small amount of the water in which they soaked, sugar, and spice into a saucepan and cook for 10 minutes.

2. Prepare piecrust.

3. Line a 9-inch plate with pastry.

4. Arrange prepared apples in pie plate. Add juice if stewed. Dot with butter. Add salt, lemon peel, and brandy or rosewater, if desired: Cover with top crust, make slits to let steam escape.

5. Bake in 350°F oven for 1 hour if stewed apples are used or 1¼ hours for uncooked fruit.

Hearth Method:

1. To prepare apples, follow one of these three methods:

a. Peel and slice apples; toss with sugar and spice until all are coated.

b. To stew apples, peel and core whole apples, then slice into rings. Put in a small hanging kettle with 1 inch of water on the bottom, sugar, and spices. Simmer over hot fire for 10 minutes.

c. Put dried apples in a bowl and cover with water. They will swell up in a couple of hours if left in a warm place, such as on a trivet near the fire. Put apples, a small amount of the water in which they soaked, sugar, and spice into a hanging kettle over a hot fire, and cook for about 10 minutes.

2. Follow Steps 2 and 3 of the Modern Method recipe.

3. Bake in a hot preheated brick oven for 50 minutes. Or preheat Dutch oven and heap coals on lid and beneath and bake for about 50 minutes or a little longer.

Yield: one 9-inch pie

Lemon Pie with Molasses

Piecrust for double-crust pie
(recipe on page 135)

1½ lemons

2 eggs

⅓ cup sugar

¾ cup molasses

"Take one lemon and a half, cut them up fine, one cup of molasses, half a cup of sugar, two eggs; mix them together, prepare your plate, with a crust in the bottom, put in half the materials, lay over a crust, then put in the rest of the materials, and cover the whole with another crust."

—*The New England Economical Housekeeper*, 1845

Modern Method:

1. Prepare piecrust and divide into three parts—two larger and one smaller. The larger ones will be for the top and bottom crust; the middle crust should just fit within the pie plate and may be supplemented with scraps from the upper and lower crusts. Roll out the bottom crust and place in baking dish; roll out the top crust and cover.

2. Cut lemon into very thin slices, remove seeds, and chop peel very fine, taking care not to spill the juice.

3. Beat eggs and add sugar, then molasses and chopped lemon and juice.

4. Pour half of the mixture into the pie plate; cover with the smaller amount of crust; pour the remaining filling and cover it with the remaining crust. Flute edges securely and prick in a pattern to allow steam to escape.

5. Bake 1 hour at 350°F.

Hearth Method:

1. Follow Steps 1–4 in the Modern Method recipe, using a redware pie plate.

2. Preheat a bake-kettle and lid 15 minutes. Bake 1 hour, changing coals after 25 minutes of baking.

Yield: one 9-inch pie

Rhubarb Stalks or Persian Apple Pie

"Rhubarb stalks, or the Persian apple, is the earliest ingredient for pies, which the spring offers. The skin should be carefully stripped, and the stalks cut into small bits, and stewed very tender. These are dear pies, for they take an enormous quantity of sugar. Seasoned like apple pies. Always remember it is more easy to add seasoning than to diminish it."

—The American Frugal Housewife, 1832

8 cups rhubarb, cut in 1-inch pieces, peeled if desired

1¾ cup brown sugar, or 1 cup white and ¾ cup brown

¼ teaspoon cloves

1 teaspoon cinnamon

½ recipe Piecrust (recipe on page 135)

Modern Method:

1. Combine rhubarb, sugar, and spices, and simmer ½ hour until tender. Heat must be very low so that sugar does not burn.
2. Prepare piecrust. Line a 9-inch pie plate with pastry.
3. Pour cooked fruit into crust.
4. Bake in 400°F oven 40 minutes.

Hearth Method:

1. Follow Step 1 in the Modern Method recipe, using a hanging kettle over a very slow fire, or hanging high over the fire.
2. Follow Steps 2–4 in the Modern Method recipe.
3. Bake in a hot brick oven or preheated Dutch oven for 40 minutes, with coals on lid and beneath.

Yield: one 9-inch pie

Marlborough Pudding

6 tablespoons butter

Juice of 1 lemon

¾ cup stewed, pureed apples

¾ cup sherry

½ cup heavy cream

¾ cup white sugar

4 eggs

½ recipe for Puff Pastry for Filled Turnovers (recipe on page 150)

2 teaspoon grated nutmeg (or to taste)

"Take 12 spoons of stewed apples, 12 of wine, 12 of sugar, 12 of melted butter and 12 of beaten eggs, a little cream, spice to your taste; lay in paste No.3, in a deep dish; bake one hour and a quarter."

—*American Cookery*, 1796

Modern Method:

1. Melt butter and set aside to cool.

2. Squeeze lemon and remove seeds.

3. Add lemon to stewed apples, sherry, cream, and sugar and mix well.

4. Add melted butter to mixture, blending well.

5. Beat eggs and add to mixture.

6. Prepare puff pastry. Line deep, 8-inch pie plate with pastry.

7. Season with grated nutmeg and spoon mixture into prepared pie plate.

8. Bake 15 minutes at 400°F. Reduce heat to 350°F and bake 45 minutes more or until a knife inserted in the center comes out clean. Cool before serving.

Hearth Method:

1. Using a redware bowl over hot coals, melt the butter and set aside to cool.

2. Follow Steps 2–7 in the Modern Method recipe.

3. Bake 1 hour in hot bake-oven, or preheated Dutch oven, with coals on lid and below.

Yield: one 8-inch deep-dish pie

"Had we children been asked what we expected on Thanksgiving Day we should have clapped our hands and said that we expected a good dinner. As we had a good dinner every day of our lives this answer shows simply that children respect symbols and types. And indeed there were certain peculiarities in the Thanksgiving dinner which there were not on common days. For instance, there was always a great deal of talk about the Marlborough pies or the Marlborough pudding. To this hour, in any old and well-regulated family in New England, you will find there is a traditional method of making the Marlborough pie, which is a sort of lemon pie, and each good housekeeper thinks that her grandmother left a better receipt for Marlborough pie than anybody else did. We had Marlborough pies at other times, but we were sure to have them on Thanksgiving Day; and it ought to be said that there was no other day on which we had four kinds of pies on the table and plum pudding beside, not to say chicken pie. In those early days ice creams or sherbets or any other kickshaws of that variety would have been spurned from a Thanksgiving dinner."

—Edward Everett Hale, *A New England Boyhood*, 1893

Puff Pastry for Filled Turnovers

PASTRY:
2 cups butter

3½ cups flour, measured after sifting

½ cup cold water

FILLING:
Jam or preserves of your choice

"Take an equal quantity of flour and butter, rub rather more than half the flour into one third of the butter, then add cold water to make it into a stiff paste. Make it round and roll it out. Dot half of the remaining butter over pastry, sift flour over it, roll up pastry, flour board and rolling pin, and roll it out. Repeat once or twice until all the butter is used.

"Roll out puff paste nearly a quarter of an inch thick and with a small saucer or a tin cutter of that size, cut it into round pieces; place upon one side raspberry or strawberry jam, or any sort of preserved fruit or stewed apples; wet the edges, fold over the other side, and press it round with the finger and thumb. Or cut the paste in the form of a diamond, lay on the fruit, and fold over the paste, so as to give it a triangular shape."

—*The Good Housekeeper*, 1839

1. Blend ²/₃ cup butter and 2 cups of flour.
2. Add ½ cup cold water, stirring gradually.
3. Roll out on a floured board. Dot with half the remaining butter, sprinkle with ¾ cup of remaining flour, dusting some on rolling pin, and roll up like a jelly roll.
4. Roll this out and repeat to use up the flour and butter.

Note: Try this with filling for mince or cranberry pie.

Modern Method:

1. Roll out puff pastry to ¼-inch thickness, cut into circles or diamonds.

2. Place a spoonful of jam, preserves, or other filling on one side of pastry. Wet the edges and fold over to form a crescent or triangle. Seal firmly.

3. Bake at 400°F for 8–10 minutes or until lightly browned.

Hearth Method:

1. Preheat oven for 2 hours.

2. Follow Steps 1 and 2 of the Modern Method recipe.

3. Bake for 10 minutes, or until lightly browned.

Yield: 20–24 servings

Apple Charlotte

8 slices stale bread

¾ cup milk

3 cups apple slices

½ cup sugar

1 teaspoon cinnamon or nutmeg, if desired

2 tablespoons butter

"Cut a sufficient number of thin slices of white bread to cover the bottom and line the sides of a baking-dish, first rubbing it thickly with butter. Put thin slices of apples into the dish in layers, till the dish is full, strewing sugar and bits of butter between. In the meantime; soak as many thin slices of bread as will cover the whole, in warm milk; over which place a plate, and a weight, to keep the bread close upon the apples. Let it bake slowly for three hours. For a middling-sized dish, you should use half a pound of butter for the whole."

—*The Cook's Own Book*, 1832

Modern Method:

1. Butter a 9-inch pie plate or a 1½-quart baking dish with a heavy lid.
2. Dip 4 slices of bread into milk and line the bottom and sides of the baking dish with the bread.
3. Layer apples, sugar, spice, and dots of butter until dish is filled.
4. Dip remaining bread into milk and arrange on top of apples. Filling will be quite high.
5. Cover with lid or ovenproof plate to press down the top layers of apples and bread.
6. Bake in a 350°F oven for ½ hour or a little more until apples are soft when tested with a knife. Serve hot or cold.

Hearth Method:

1. Follow Steps 1–5 in the Modern Method recipe.
2. Bake on a trivet in a moderate bake-oven or in a Dutch oven for ½ hour or a little more.

Yield: 8 servings

COMMON CAKES

"In all cakes where butter and eggs are used, the butter should be very faithfully rubbed into the flour and the eggs beat to a foam, before the ingredients are mixed."

—The American Frugal Housewife, 1832

A Note on Flour

Wheat did not grow well in most of New England in the early 1800s, but to most people's palates wheat made the best bread. An elastic protein called gluten found in wheat flour dough trapped tiny carbon dioxide bubbles given off by yeast. This made for a lighter loaf. Most people preferred white bread for social as well as culinary reasons.

In the early 1800s, most of the wheat New Englanders ate came from the mid-Atlantic states, and newly opened lands in Ohio and upstate New York. They bought it as flour in barrels. It came in different grades, depending on fineness and whiteness. It differed somewhat from most flours available today. For one thing, it was made from a soft white variety of wheat and resembled modern pastry flour. Bread flours today are generally milled from hard red wheat and are higher in gluten. (The color refers to the outer bran layer, now completely removed in milling.) Modern flours are made with steel rollers and screens that not only completely remove the fibrous outer bran layer but also the oil-rich germ (an embryonic wheat plant), leaving only the starchy endosperm as flour. In the early 1800s flat round millstones left the bran and germ mixed in the flour. Sifting through fine silk reels called bolters removed larger flakes of the bran, but some specks of fine bran and all of the germ remained in the flour. The oils in the germ began to turn rancid within months, and as a result this flour spoiled faster than modern flour.

Freshly ground flour has a slight yellow/green tint to it and does not rise as well as flour that has been oxidized by age. In the 1800s this meant that flour baked better after a few weeks than when freshly ground. Today this process is accomplished instantaneously in the mill by a process called bleaching. (Bleaching cannot change the color of any bran flakes.) Contemporary flour is also "fortified," i.e. the vitamins removed by taking out the perishable germ are artificially added back in. Of course, no one knew about vitamins until the twentieth century! Modern flours often also have some barley flour or ground barley malt added to the wheat, primarily to enhance their baking qualities. Flours today are also "pre-sifted." While sifting (to remove bran and isolate the finest particles) is what distinguishes flour from a fine meal (ground but not sifted), flours in the 1800s lacked anti-caking agents commonly added to modern flours, and required a second sifting by the baker to ensure a uniform product. Sifting also served as a form of quality control, removing any insects or other impurities that might have made their way into the flour. In the 1800s there were occasional complaints that flour was being adulterated with alum or plaster to make it whiter; this may have been true in some cases, but not in most.

Cup Cake

"Cup cake is about as good as pound cake, and is cheaper. One cup of butter, two cups of sugar, three cups of flour, and four eggs, well beat together, and baked in pans or cups. Bake twenty minutes, and no more."

—*The American Frugal Housewife,* 1832

1 cup butter

2 cups sugar

4 eggs

3 cups flour, measured after sifting

Modern Method:

1. Cream butter and sugar thoroughly.

2. Beat eggs and blend into creamed butter and sugar.

3. Add flour and beat in for 2 minutes.

4. If using cupcake or muffin pans or ovenproof cups (like custard cups), grease and flour and fill each cup ½ to ²/₃ full. Bake at 375°F for 20 minutes.

5. If using a round cake pan, grease and flour. Bake at 375°F for 45 minutes.

Hearth Method:

1. Using your hand as a tool, rub the butter into the flour until well blended. Add sugar to the mixture.

2. Beat eggs and blend into mixture. Beat well using either your hand or a strong wooden spoon.

3. If using cupcake or muffin pans or ovenproof cups (like custard cups), grease and flour and fill each cup ½ to ²/₃ full. Place a trivet on the floor of the bake oven, as cupcakes will burn if tin muffin pans are placed directly in a brick oven.

4. Bake for 20 minutes in a preheated brick oven or Dutch oven with coals below and on the lid.

Yield: 20–24 cupcakes or 1 round cake

Hard Gingerbread (Cookies)

1/3 cup boiling water

1 teaspoon baking soda

3/4 cup molasses

1 teaspoon ginger

2 1/4 cups sifted flour

"Take a tea-cupful of molasses, a tea-spoonful of saleratus dissolved in half a cup of boiling water, a teaspoonful of ginger, and flour to make it hard enough to roll. Bake it five minutes."

—The New England Economical Housekeeper, 1845

Modern Method:

1. Pour boiling water into a large mixing bowl and add baking soda, then molasses. When mixed, add ginger.
2. Add flour gradually and work into a soft dough. Chill 15 minutes or more.
3. Take about half the dough at a time and roll out on a floured board. Cut into small circles or desired shapes.
4. Bake on a greased cookie sheet in a 350°F oven for 8 minutes. Thick or large cookies will take a little longer.

Hearth Method:

1. Follow Steps 1–3 of the Modern Method recipe.
2. Bake on greased pottery plates, 5 minutes in a brick oven, slightly longer in a Dutch oven, changing coals after every second batch.

Yield: 30 cookies

"If you have breakfasted early, it will be well to put some ginger bread nuts or biscuits into your satchel, as you may become very hungry before dinner."

—Eliza Leslie,
The Behaviour Book (Philadelphia, 1854)

Soft Gingerbread

"Six tea cups of flour, three of molasses, one of cream, one of butter, one table-spoonful of ginger and one of saleratus."

—The New England Economical Housekeeper, 1845

4½ cups flour
1 tablespoon ginger
1 tablespoon baking soda
¾ cup butter
¾ cup cream
2¼ cups molasses

Modern Method:

1. Sift together flour, ginger, and baking soda.

2. Cut butter into dry ingredients and blend thoroughly.

3. Stir in cream and molasses.

4. Grease two 8-inch or 9-inch square pans. Bake 45 minutes at 300°F.

Hearth Method:

1. Follow Steps 1–3 in the Modern Method recipe.

2. Use greased pottery pie plates or cast-iron pans. Baking time in preheated brick oven or Dutch oven will range from 30 to 45 minutes depending on size of pan and depth of batter.

Yield: 12–18 servings

Election Cake

1 cup yeast, or 2 packages yeast with 1 cup warm water and 1 tablespoon sugar (recipe on page 181)

¾ cup butter

1 cup sugar

2 eggs

7–8 cups sifted flour

½ pound currants or raisins

1 cup milk, or more

"Old-fashioned election cake is made of four pounds of flour; three quarters of a pound of butter; four eggs; one pound of sugar; one pound of currants, or raisins if you choose; half a pint of good yeast; wet it with milk as soft as it can be and be moulded on a board. Set to rise over night in winter; in warm weather, three hours is usually enough for it to rise. A loaf, the size of common flour bread, should bake three quarters of an hour."

—*The American Frugal Housewife*, 1832

Modern Method:

1. If packaged yeast is used, mix water and sugar with yeast.
2. Cream butter and sugar. Add eggs, beating after each addition. Add yeast and blend well.
3. Stir in 4 cups flour and beat 1 minute.
4. Combine currants or raisins with 3 cups remaining flour and add to rest of batter. Batter will be stiff and flour may need to be worked in by hand. Add milk as required to make a soft yet kneadable dough.
5. Sprinkle remaining flour on a board. Knead for 10 minutes.
6. Divide dough in half. Use 5-by-9-inch loaf pans or two 8-inch pie plates. Let rise in greased pans in a warm place for 3–5 hours or overnight in the refrigerator.
7. Bake in preheated 350°F oven for 50 minutes.

Hearth Method:

1. Follow Steps 1–5 in the Modern Method recipe.

2. Divide dough in half. To bake in brick oven or Dutch oven, use cast-iron or ceramic pans, 5-by-9-inch loaf pans, or two 8-inch pie plates. Set in front of the fire or in any warm place to rise. The cake will rise in 2 hours in front of the fire while the oven preheats. Allow 3–5 hours to rise in a less warm place or let rise overnight in a cool place or refrigerator.

3. Bake in a hot preheated brick oven for 45 minutes.

Yield: two loaves or rounds

"Old Election, 'Lection Day as we called it, a lost holiday now, was a general training day, and it came at our most delightful season, the last of May. Lilacs and tulips were in bloom.... My mother always made 'Lection cake for us on that day. It was nothing but a kind of sweetened bread with a slice of egg and molasses on top; but we thought it delicious."

—Lucy Larcom,
A New England Girlhood (Boston, 1889)

Wedding Cake

FULL RECIPE:

2 pounds raisins

1 cup brandy

12 cups flour

4 tablespoons mace

2 tablespoons grated nutmeg

4 pounds currants

8 ounces citron, optional

3 pounds butter

6 cups sugar

2 dozen eggs

½ cup molasses

¼ RECIPE:

½ pound raisins

¼ cup brandy

3 cups flour

1 tablespoon mace

2 teaspoons nutmeg

1 pound currants

2 ounces citron, optional

¾ pound butter

1½ cups sugar

"Good common wedding cake may be made thus: Four pounds of flour, three pounds of butter, three pounds of sugar, four pounds of currants, two pounds of raisins, twenty-four eggs, half a pint of brandy, or lemon-brandy, one ounce of mace, and three nutmegs. A little molasses makes it dark colored, which is desirable. Half a pound of citron improves it; but is not necessary. To be baked two hours and a half, or three hours. After the oven is cleared, it is well to shut the door for eight or ten minutes, to let the violence of the heat subside, before cake or bread is put in.

"To make icing for your wedding cake, beat the whites of eggs to an entire froth, and to each egg add five teaspoonfuls of sifted loaf sugar, gradually; beat it a great while. Put it on when your cake is hot, or cold, as is most convenient. It will dry in a warm room, a short distance from a gentle fire, or in a warm oven."

—*The American Frugal Housewife*, 1832

Note: The full recipe will make 14 pounds of cake, which can be baked in different-size pans to build up a tiered wedding cake. A very fruity and spicy cake with the combination of nutmeg and mace, this requires a very large bake-oven or a combination of ovens and kettles.

Modern Method:

1. Soak raisins in brandy overnight.
2. Sift flour before measuring. Sift flour with spices, and add currants and citron, if desired.
3. Cream butter and sugar. Add eggs one at a time, beating to blend after each addition. Stir in molasses and any brandy that was not absorbed by the raisins. Stir in sifted flour with spices and fruits.
4. Grease two 5-by-9-inch loaf pans, three 8-inch round pans, or one 10-inch tube pan.

5. Pour batter into greased pans and bake about 2 hours or a little more in 350°F oven.

Hearth Method:

1. Follow Steps 1–3 in the Modern Method recipe.
2. Pour batter into three greased pottery or ceramic baking pans and bake 2¼ hours in a preheated hot bake-oven.

Modern and Hearth Methods:

1. Beat egg whites. Add sugar, beating until smooth and white.
2. Spread icing over slightly warm cake. It will harden very slowly. Set cake back into oven to begin drying as the oven cools down.

Yield: full recipe: 14 pounds of cake
    ¼ recipe: one 10-inch tube cake, or two 5-by-9-inch loaves, or three 8-inch layers

6 eggs

2 tablespoons molasses

ICING (FOR ¼ RECIPE
WEDDING CAKE):
3 egg whites

1 cup powdered granulated
sugar (not superfine)

(For full recipe quadruple the
¼ recipe amount)

Sponge Cake

6 eggs, separated

2¼ cups sugar

2¼ cups flour, sifted

"The nicest way to make sponge cake, or diet-bread, is the weight of six eggs in sugar, the weight of four eggs in flour, a little rosewater. The whites and yolks should be beaten thoroughly and separately. The eggs and sugar should be well beaten together; but after the flour is sprinkled, it should not be stirred a moment longer than is necessary to mix it well; it should be poured into the pan, and got into the oven with all possible expedition. Twenty minutes is about long enough to bake. Not to be put in till some other articles have taken off the first few minutes of furious heat."

—The American Frugal Housewife, 1832

Modern Method:

1. Beat egg whites until stiff.
2. Beat egg yolks and add sugar gradually, beating until thick and lemon colored.
3. Gently fold yolks into whites.
4. Sift flour over the batter and fold in gently.
5. Grease and flour two 8-inch or 9-inch layer cake pans or a 9-inch tube pan. Spoon batter into pan.
6. Bake at 375°F for 50–55 minutes.

Hearth Method:

1. Follow Steps 1–4 in the Modern Method recipe.
2. Grease and flour three 8-inch or 9-inch pottery pie plates or two large, straight-sided ceramic baking dishes, such as a soufflé dish. Spoon batter into plate or dish.
3. Bake in a hot brick oven for 45–50 minutes.

Yield: two 8-inch or 9-inch layers or one 9-inch tube cake

Doughnuts

"For dough-nuts, take one pint of flour, half a pint of sugar, three eggs, a piece of butter as big as an egg, and a tea-spoonful of dissolved pearlash. When you have no eggs, a gill of lively emptings will do; but in that case, they must be made over night. Cinnamon, rose-water, or lemon-brandy, if you have it. If you use part lard instead of butter, add a little salt. Not put in till the fat is very hot. The more fat they are fried in, the less they will soak fat."

—The American Frugal Housewife, 1832

4 tablespoons butter

1 cup sugar

3 eggs

2 cups flour

1 teaspoon baking powder

1 teaspoon cinnamon

Fat for deep-frying

Modern Method:

1. Cream butter and sugar.

2. Add eggs one at a time and beat well.

3. Sift and measure flour, then stir in baking powder and cinnamon.

4. Knead gently until ingredients are blended.

5. Pull dough apart and roll into 1-inch balls, no larger or centers will not cook before crust is thoroughly brown.

6. Preheat fat to 375°F in an electric fryer or melt and warm fat on top of stove. The fat is hot enough when a small pinch of dough dropped in rises to the surface of the fat immediately.

7. Slip doughnuts carefully into the hot fat. Do not crowd. Turn when underside has browned. Drain on paper towels.

Hearth Method:

1. Follow Steps 1–5 in the Modern Method recipe.

2. Follow Step 6 in the Modern Method recipe, using a hanging skillet.

3. Follow Step 7 in the Modern Method recipe, pulling the skillet away from fire when putting doughnuts into the fat.

Yield: 4 dozen

Pancakes

2 eggs

1 cup milk

2 cups flour, measured after sifting

3 tablespoons sugar

1 teaspoon baking powder

½ teaspoon cinnamon

⅛ teaspoon ground cloves

¼ teaspoon salt

Fat for deep-frying

"Pancakes should be made of half a pint of milk, three great spoonfuls of sugar, one or two eggs, a tea-spoonful of dissolved pearlash, spiced with cinnamon, or cloves, a little salt, rose-water, or lemon-brandy, just as you happen to have it. Flour should be stirred in till the spoon moves round with difficulty. If they are thin, they are apt to soak fat. Have the fat in your skillet boiling hot, and drop them in with a spoon. Let them cook till thoroughly brown. The fat which is left is good to shorten other cakes. The more fat they are cooked in, the less they soak."

—*The American Frugal Housewife,* 1832

Modern Method:

1. Beat eggs and add milk. Set aside.

2. In a large mixing bowl combine flour, sugar, baking powder, spices, and salt.

3. Pour milk and egg mixture into center of dry ingredients and stir quickly.

4. Heat oil or fat for frying in a deep skillet or deep fat fryer, 375°F in an electric fryer. The fat is hot enough when a small pinch of dough dropped in rises to the surface of the fat immediately.

5. Drop batter into the fat by tablespoons, leaving enough room for the pancakes to swell as they cook. When one side is browned, about 5 minutes, turn to brown other side.

6. Drain on paper towels. Serve warm with butter and maple syrup.

Hearth Method:

1. Follow Steps 1–3 in the Modern Method recipe.

2. Follow Step 4 in the Modern Method recipe, using a hanging skillet.

3. Pull skillet forward to drop batter into the fat. Push back over fire to brown, about 5 minutes. Turn pancake to brown other side.

4. Follow Step 6 in the Modern Method recipe.

Yield: 48

"There were such nice waffles (in the picnic basket) as nobody could bake but Grandma and such tender cold tongue, and dainty delicate slices of boiled ham and such nice cakes and comfits."

—Ellen Louise Chandler,
"A Husking Party at Ryefield," *This, That and The Other* (Boston, 1854)

Apple Pancakes

2 cups sour milk or 1¾ cups fresh milk with 2 tablespoons lemon juice

¾ cup cornmeal

2 apples

¾ cup molasses

1 teaspoon baking soda

2–2½ cups sifted flour

Fat for deep-frying

Butter

"One pint of sour milk, a tea-spoonful of saleratus, a tea-cup of fine Indian meal, a tea-cup of molasses, three sweet apples chopped fine and mixed in, and flour enough to make the right thickness to drop from a spoon. Have your fat boiling hot. Cook till they slip from the fork."

—The New England Economical Housekeeper, 1845

Modern Method:

1. Mix milk and cornmeal.
2. Chop apples and stir into milk and cornmeal. Add molasses and baking soda.
3. Stir in flour.
4. Heat fat for frying in deep skillet or deep-fat fryer, 375°F in an electric fryer. The fat is hot enough when a small pinch of dough dropped in rises to the surface of the fat immediately.
5. Drop batter into the fat by tablespoonfuls, leaving enough room for the pancakes to swell as they cook. When one side is browned, about 3–5 minutes, turn pancake to brown other side.
6. Drain on paper towels. Serve warm with butter.

Hearth Method:

1. Follow Steps 1–3 in the Modern Method recipe.
2. Heat fat in hanging skillet and follow Steps 4 and 5 in the Modern Method recipe. Pull away from fire when adding batter or turning pancakes. Turn when browned on first side.
3. Follow Step 6 in the Modern Method recipe.

Yield: 5 dozen

Fritters

"Flat-jacks, or fritters, do not differ from pancakes, only in being mixed softer. The same ingredients are used in about the same quantities; only most people prefer to have no sweetening put in them, because they generally have butter, sugar, and nutmeg put on them, after they are done. Excepting for company, the nutmeg can be well dispensed with. They are not to be boiled in fat, like pancakes; the spider or griddle should be well greased, and the cakes poured on as large as you want them, when it is quite hot; when it gets brown on one side, to be turned over upon the other. Fritters are better to be baked quite thin. Either flour, Indian, or rye, is good."

—*The American Frugal Housewife*, 1832

2 eggs

1 cup milk

1½ cups flour or cornmeal, measured after sifting

1 teaspoon baking powder

½ teaspoon cinnamon

⅛ teaspoon ground cloves

¼ teaspoon salt

5 tablespoons sugar

Fat to grease skillet

1 teaspoon nutmeg

Butter

Note: Fritters in the nineteenth century were cooked in a similar process to that of modern pancakes, whereas pancakes were deep fried like modern fritters. The terms were later reversed.

Modern Method:

1. Beat eggs and milk together.
2. Sift flour with baking powder, cinnamon, cloves, salt, and 2 tablespoons sugar. Stir quickly into egg and milk mixture.
3. Preheat skillet or griddle. When hot, grease, and drop 2–3 tablespoons batter for each fritter onto skillet. Turn when first side is browned. Grease griddle lightly after every two or three batches.
4. Combine 3 tablespoons sugar and nutmeg. Serve fritter with butter and nutmeg-sugar.

Hearth Method:

Follow Steps 1–4 of the Modern Method recipe, using a hanging skillet.

Yield: 16–18

Short Cake

¼ cup butter, shortening, or sour milk

2 cups flour

1 teaspoon baking soda

¾ cup sour milk or buttermilk

"If you have sour milk, or butter-milk, it is well to make it into short cakes for tea. Rub in a very small bit of shortening, or three table-spoonfuls of cream, with the flour; put in a tea-spoonful of strong dissolved pearlash, into your sour milk, and mix your cake pretty stiff, to bake in the spider, on a few embers. When people have to buy butter and lard, short cakes are not economical food. A half-pint of flour will make a cake large enough to cover a common plate. Knead it stiff enough to roll well, to bake in a plate or in a spider. It should bake as quick as it can and not burn. The first side should stand longer to the fire than the last."

—The American Frugal Housewife, 1832

Modern Method:

1. Blend butter, shortening, or sour milk with 1¾ cups flour.
2. Stir soda into sour milk or buttermilk and mix with flour mixture. Batter will be sticky.
3. Sprinkle remaining ¼ cup of flour over a board and knead for less than a minute. Roll dough to the size of an 8-inch or 9-inch pie plate and place it in the plate.
4. Bake in 425°F oven for 10–12 minutes.

Hearth Method:

1. Follow Steps 1–3 in the Modern Method recipe, rolling dough to the size of the spider or plate to be used.
2. Bake in a preheated spider over hot coals. After 5 minutes, turn and bake 3–4 minutes on the other side. Or bake on a pie plate or flat plate on a trivet over coals, turning after 5–6 minutes and cooking 3–4 minutes on the other side.

Yield: one 8-inch or 9-inch cake

Indian Cake

"Indian cake, or bannock is sweet and cheap food. Two cups of Indian meal, one table-spoonful molasses, two cups milk, a little salt, a handful flour, a little saleratus, mixed up thin, and poured into a buttered bake-kettle, hung over the fire uncovered, until you can bear your finger upon it, and then set down before the fire. Bake half an hour. A little stewed pumpkin, scalded with the meal improves the cake. Bannock split and dipped in butter makes very nice toast."

—*The American Frugal Housewife*, 1832

1½ cups cornmeal

1½ cups very hot milk

½ cup cooked pumpkin, optional

1 tablespoon molasses

¼ cup flour

1 teaspoon salt

2 teaspoons baking soda

¼ cup butter or lard

Butter

Modern Method:

1. Scald cornmeal by pouring hot milk over it gradually, stirring to blend. Stir in cooked pumpkin, if desired. When the milk is absorbed, and mixture has cooled, continue with the recipe.

2. Stir molasses into scalded cornmeal. Add flour, salt, and baking soda.

3. Preheat a 9-inch cast-iron skillet and melt butter or lard in it on top of stove. Pour in batter and stir constantly while it cooks. In 5 minutes or less it will be firm.

4. Remove from heat immediately. Spread the batter evenly in the skillet and smooth the top with the back of a spoon.

5. Bake in the oven at 350°F for ½ hour, no more.

6. Serve warm, or after it cools, split and toast. Serve with butter.

Hearth Method:

1. Follow Steps 1 and 2 in the Modern Method recipe.

2. Preheat hanging skillet and melt butter or lard. Pour in batter and stir constantly while it cooks. In about 10–15 minutes it will be firm.

3. Follow Step 4 in the Modern Method recipe.

4. Prop skillet against a brick or other heavy object so that the dough is facing the heat of the fire to bake for ½ hour.

5. Follow Step 6 in the Modern Method recipe.

Yield: one 9-inch cake

Washington Cake

¾ cup butter

1 cup sugar

3 eggs

¼ cup wine

2½–3 cups flour, measured after sifting

1 teaspoon baking soda

2 teaspoons nutmeg

1½ teaspoon cinnamon

½ pint heavy cream or sour milk

"Beat together 1½ pounds of sugar, and three quarters of a pound of butter; add 4 eggs well beaten, half pint of sour milk, and 1 teaspoonful of saleratus, dissolved in a little hot water. Stir in gradually 1¾ pounds of flour, 1 wine glassful of wine or brandy, and 1 nutmeg grated. Beat all well together. This will make two round cakes. It should be baked in a quick oven, and will take from 15 to 30 minutes, according to the thickness of the cakes."

—The Ladies' New Book of Cookery, 1852

Modern Method:

1. Cream butter and sugar until light.

2. Beat eggs, add wine. Combine with butter and sugar mixture.

3. Sift together flour, baking soda, and spices.

4. Add ⅓ of the flour mixture and ½ of the cream, then add ⅓ of the flour mixture and the remaining cream, and then add the remaining flour mixture, blending well after each addition.

5. Grease two 8-inch round cake pans, pour in batter, and bake for 45 minutes, or use a tube pan and bake for 70 minutes, at 350°F.

Hearth Method:

1. Follow Steps 1–4 in the Modern Method recipe.

2. Put batter in two 9-inch pottery pie plates or two round, straight-sided oven-proof dishes of 8–9 inches in diameter. Bake for 1¼ hours in a moderate bake-oven.

Yield: two 8-inch or 9-inch layers, or one tube cake

"After the oration came another national salute—thirteen guns, one for each of the original states . . . a feu de joie from the old flint lock muskets of the militia and then an attack upon the bread and cheese & rum punch provided by the committee."

—Francis M. Thompson,
History of Greenfield, Shire Town of Franklin County (Greenfield, 1904)

Jumbles

1 cup butter

1 cup granulated sugar

3 eggs

1 tablespoon rosewater or lemon extract

2 cups flour, measured after sifting

1 tablespoon nutmeg

½ teaspoon mace

½ teaspoon cinnamon

1 cup powdered sugar

"Three eggs, half a pound of flour sifted, half a pound of butter, half a pound of powdered loaf-sugar, a table-spoonful of rose-water, a nutmeg grated, a tea-spoonful of mixed mace and cinnamon. Stir the butter to a cream. Beat the eggs very light. Throw them, all at once, into the pan of flour. Put in, at once, the butter and sugar, and then add the spice and rose-water. If you have no rose-water, substitute six or seven drops of strong essence of lemon, or more if the essence is weak. Stir the whole very hard, with a knife.

"Spread some flour on your paste-board, and flour your hands well. Take up with your knife, a portion of the dough, and lay it on the board. Roll it lightly with your hands, into long thin rolls, which must be cut into equal lengths, curled up into rings, and laid gently into an iron or tin pan, buttered, not too close to each other, as they spread in baking. Bake them in a quick oven about five minutes, and grate loaf-sugar over them when cool."

—*Seventy-Five Receipts,* 1830

Note: The word *jumble* was used as early as 1615 to describe sweet cakes. It is probably taken from *gimbal*, a twisted double finger ring popular at the time, because the cookie's shape resembled the ring. The derivation of *gimbal* is from the Latin *gemellus*, for twin.

Modern Method:

1. Cream butter and sugar.

2. Beat eggs and rosewater or lemon extract until light and blend into butter and sugar mixture.

3. Sift flour and spices; add to egg mixture, stirring until blended. If dough is very soft, chill for 2 hours.

4. On a lightly floured board, roll dough with the palm of your hand into strips of ¼–½ inch in diameter. Cut into 6-inch lengths and form into a double circle shape, similar to a pretzel. Place 1 inch apart on a lightly greased baking sheet to allow for expansion.

5. Bake 8–10 minutes in 375°F oven.

6. When cool, sift powdered sugar over jumbles or shake a few cookies at a time in a bag with powdered sugar.

Hearth Method:

1. Follow Steps 1–4 in the Modern Method recipe.

2. If using metal cookie sheets in a brick oven, place on trivets. Bake in a hot oven for 8–10 minutes. Small cakes with a short cooking time can be baked more easily in a Dutch oven on a pottery pie plate. Change coals after every second batch.

3. Follow Step 6 in the Modern Method recipe.

Yield: 3–4 dozen

Wafers

1/4 pound butter

4 eggs

1/2 cup sugar

1/2 teaspoon mace

1 1/4 cups sifted flour

Large pat of butter

2 cups whipped cream

Strawberry preserves, frozen whole strawberries, or other fruits (try with Red Currant Cream, page 115, or Quince Cream with Ginger, page 118)

"Dry the flour well which you intend to use, mix a little pounded sugar and finely pounded mace with it, then make it into a thick batter with cream; butter the wafer irons, let them be hot, put a teaspoonful of batter into them, so bake them carefully, and roll them off the iron with a stick.

"If you are preparing for company, fill up the hollow of the wafers with whipt cream, and stop up the two ends with preserved strawberries or with any other small sweetmeat."
—*A New System of Domestic Cookery*, 1807

Modern Method:

1. Preheat pizzelle or krumkake iron (on the stove) according to manufacturer's instructions while batter is mixed.

2. Melt 1/4 pound butter.

3. Beat eggs; add sugar, mace, and melted butter.

4. Add flour and blend.

5. Remove iron from heat; place on pads or towels to protect table. Wrap a lump of butter in a clean cloth and brush lightly over both sides of iron to grease it.

6. Place 1 tablespoon of batter in center of iron, and leave for about 30 seconds. Remove immediately. Two wafers can be made before iron has to be reheated.

7. While still warm and pliable, roll wafers into cylinders using the handle of a wooden spoon. Allow to cool. Spoon whipped cream into hollow and garnish with fruit or preserves.

Hearth Method:

1. Preheat wafer iron in glowing coals while batter is mixed.

2. To mix, cook, and serve, follow Steps 2–7 in Modern Method recipe.

Yield: 30–36 wafers

Wafer Iron

Macaroons

2²/₃ cups ground almonds

1 teaspoon rosewater

2 cups granulated sugar

8 egg whites

2 cups sifted flour

"Beat to a froth the whites of 8 eggs, then add 2 pounds finely pounded and sifted loaf sugar, one pound of blanched sweet almonds, which must be pounded to a paste with rose water. Beat all these together till they become a thick paste, then drop it from a spoon upon a buttered tin. Place the drops a little apart as they may spread. Bake them about 10 minutes in a moderate oven. Cocoanut cakes may be made in the same manner substituting for the pounded almonds ½ pound finely grated cocoanut."

—Seventy-Five Receipts, 1830

Modern Method:

1. Grind almonds to a paste with rosewater.
2. Grind sugar in blender or with mortar and pestle if available. Beat egg whites and gradually add sugar to them.
3. Stir in flour and almond paste.
4. Drop batter by teaspoonfuls one inch apart on buttered cookie sheet. Bake 10 minutes in 350°F oven.

Hearth Method:

1. Follow Steps 1–3 in the Modern Method recipe.
2. To bake in Dutch oven, drop batter by teaspoonfuls 1 inch apart on buttered pie plate. Bake 8–10 minutes. Change coals after every second batch.

Coconut Macaroons:

Substitute 2½ cups flaked coconut for almonds; reduce flour to 1 cup. Omit Step 1 and use flour and coconut flakes in Step 3.

Yield: 6 dozen

BREADS, YEAST, &C.

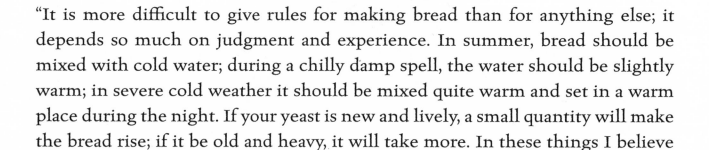

"It is more difficult to give rules for making bread than for anything else; it depends so much on judgment and experience. In summer, bread should be mixed with cold water; during a chilly damp spell, the water should be slightly warm; in severe cold weather it should be mixed quite warm and set in a warm place during the night. If your yeast is new and lively, a small quantity will make the bread rise; if it be old and heavy, it will take more. In these things I believe wisdom must be gained by a few mistakes."

—The American Frugal Housewife, 1832

Yeast

"Those who make their own bread should make yeast too. When bread is nearly out, always think whether yeast is in readiness; for it takes a day and night to prepare it. One handful of hops, with two or three handsful of malt and rye bran, should be boiled fifteen or twenty minutes, in two quarts of water, then strained, hung on to boil again, and thickened with half a pint of rye and water stirred up quite thick, and a little molasses; boil it a minute or two, and then take it off to cool. When just about lukewarm, put in a cupful of good lively yeast, and set it in a cool place in summer, and warm place in winter. If it is too warm when you put in the old yeast, all the spirit will be killed."

—*The American Frugal Housewife*, 1832

1 cup dried hops

2–3 cups whole-wheat or rye flour

2 quarts water

½ cup rye flour

1 tablespoon molasses

1 cup water

1 package commercial yeast or 1 cup reserved yeast from previous batch

Modern Method:

1. In a large pot, combine hops, flour, and water. Bring to a boil over high heat and cook for 2 minutes.
2. Strain the water off and return it to the cooking pot.
3. Make up a thick paste of rye flour, molasses, and water. Stir this into the liquid in the pot. Bring to a boil, stir, and boil again briefly. Remove from heat to cool.
4. When lukewarm, stir in 1 package commercial yeast or 1 cup reserved yeast.
5. Store loosely covered in a glass container in a cool place. It will be ready to use in 24 hours.

Hearth Method:

1. Follow Steps 1–3 in the Modern Method recipe, using a large hanging kettle over a hot fire.
2. Follow Steps 4 and 5 in the Modern Method recipe.

Yield: 8 cups liquid yeast

Flour Bread

4–5 cups flour, measured after sifting

2 packages dry yeast, dissolved in 2 cups warm water and 1 teaspoon sugar, or 1 cup homemade yeast (recipe on page 181) and 1 cup water

"Flour bread should have a sponge set the night before. The sponge should be soft enough to pour; mixed with water, warm or cold, according to the temperature of the weather. One gill of lively yeast is enough to put into sponge for two loaves. I should judge about three pints of sponge would be right for two loaves. The warmth of the place in which the sponge is set, should be determined by the coldness of the weather. If your sponge looks frothy in the morning, it is a sign your bread will be good; if it does not rise, stir in a little more empt-ings; if it rises too much, taste of it, to see if it has any acid taste; if so, put in a tea-spoonful of pearlash when you mould in your flour; be sure the pearlash is well dissolved in water; if there are little lumps, your bread will be full of bitter spots. About an hour before your oven is ready, stir in flour into your sponge till it is stiff enough to lay on a well floured board or table. Knead it up pretty stiff, and put it into well greased pans, and let it stand in a cool or warm place, according to the weather. . . . Common sized loaves will bake in three quarters of an hour. If they slip easily in the pans, it is a sign they are done."

—*The American Frugal Housewife*, 1832

Modern Method:

1. Beat together 2 cups flour and liquid yeast by hand. This is the sponge.
2. Let rise overnight in refrigerator. Bowl should be covered with a cloth.
3. Add 2–3 cups sifted flour to form a soft dough. Knead 10 minutes on board sprinkled with ¼ cup flour.
4. Divide dough in half. Grease two 8-inch or 9-inch pie plates or two 5-by-9-inch tin or ceramic loaf pans. Shape round loaves so that the dough covers the bottom of the pan. For rectangular loaves, roll out or flatten the divided dough into two 9-inch-long cylinders, and fit them from end to end in each loaf pan.
5. Let dough rise 2 hours or more until doubled in bulk.
6. Preheat oven to 400°F. Put bread in oven and reduce heat to 375°F. Bake loaves for 50 minutes.
7. Remove from pans and cool.

Hearth Method:

1. Follow Step 1 in the Modern Method recipe, beating by hand.

2. Follow Step 2 in the Modern Method recipe, letting dough rise 1½ hours on the hearth.

3. Follow Steps 3 and 4 in the Modern Method recipe. (Do not use tin loaf pans.)

4. Let dough rise until doubled in bulk. This is a good time to begin to preheat the bake-oven, as both will require about 2 hours.

5. Bake bread in hot oven for 45–50 minutes. Bread can be baked in pans or directly on the oven floor. If using the oven floor, sprinkle cornmeal on the floor of the oven and slide the bread from the plates to the oven floor.

6. Remove from pans and cool before cutting.

Yield: two 8-inch or 9-inch rounds, or two 5-by-9-inch loaves

Three-Grain Bread

4 cups boiling water

2 cups cornmeal

2 teaspoons salt

½ cup liquid yeast (recipe on page 181), or 2 packages dry yeast dissolved in ½ cup water and 1 teaspoon sugar

2¼ cups rye flour

2 cups wheat flour, measured after sifting

"Some people like one third Indian in their flour. Others like one third rye; and some think the nicest of all bread is one third Indian, one third rye and one third flour made according to the directions for flour bread.

"When Indian is used it should be salted, and scalded before the other meal is put in."

—*The American Frugal Housewife, 1832*

Modern Method:

1. To make sponge, pour boiling water over cornmeal and salt in a large mixing bowl. Let it sit until the water is absorbed. When cooled, stir in yeast and 1 cup of rye flour. To set the sponge, cover the bowl and let it rest overnight in the refrigerator. The sponge will probably look flat, but the yeast will have worked.
2. To the sponge, add the wheat flour and 1 cup rye flour.
3. Knead for 10 minutes on a board sprinkled with rye flour. Divide dough in half. Grease two 8-inch or 9-inch pie plates or two 5-by-9-inch tin or ceramic loaf pans. Shape round loaves so that the dough covers the bottom of the pan. For rectangular loaves, roll out or flatten the divided dough into two 9-inch-long cylinders, and fit them from end to end in each loaf pan.
4. Set in a warm place to rise until doubled in bulk, about 2 hours.
5. Preheat oven to 400°F. Put bread in oven and reduce heat to 375°F. Bake for 50 minutes.

Hearth Method:

1. Follow Steps 1–3 in the Modern Method recipe. Do not use tin or aluminum baking pans.
2. Set in warm place to rise until doubled in bulk. This is a good time to begin to preheat the bake-oven, as both will require about 2 hours.

3. Bake bread in a hot oven for 45–50 minutes. Bread can be baked in pans or directly on the oven floor. If using the oven floor, sprinkle cornmeal on the floor of the oven and slide the bread from the plates to the oven floor.

Yield: two 8-inch or 9-inch rounds, or two 5-by-9-inch loaves

Potato and Flour Bread

2 medium potatoes, or 1 cup leftover mashed potatoes

6–7 cups flour

2½ cups warm milk

1 teaspoon salt

1 package yeast dissolved in ¼ cup water

"Weigh half a pound of mealy potatoes after they are boiled or steamed and rub them while warm into a pound and a half of fine flour dried for a little while before the fire. When thoroughly mixed, put in a spoonful and a half of yeast, a little salt, and warm milk and water enough to work it into a dough. Let this stand by the fire to rise for an hour and a half; then make it into a loaf and bake in a moderately brisk oven. If baked in a tin the crust will be more delicate but the bread dries sooner."

—*The Experienced American Housekeeper,* 1829

Modern Method:

1. Boil 2 whole medium potatoes until fork tender. Peel and mash. Add mashed potatoes to 3 cups flour. Stir in milk, salt, and dissolved yeast. Cover and let rise until doubled in bulk, about 1½ hours.

2. Add remaining flour until dough is stiff, about 3–4 cups. Knead slightly and set in greased bread pans to rise.

3. Preheat oven to 375°F. When bread has doubled in bulk, after about 1 hour, bake for 45 minutes or until top is brown.

Hearth Method:

1. Boil potatoes in hanging kettle over fire. Follow directions in Step 1 in the recipe above.

2. Follow Step 2 in the Modern Method recipe, using round baking pans.

3. Preheat bake-kettle for 15 minutes. Bake in bake-kettle about 45 minutes, changing coals after 25 minutes of baking.

Yield: 2 loaves

Rice Bread

"Boil a pint of rice soft; add a pint of leaven; then three quarts of the flour; put it to rise in a tin or earthen vessel until it has risen sufficiently; divide it into three parts; then bake it as other bread, and you will have three large loaves."

—*The American Frugal Housewife*, 1832

1 cup rice

2 quarts water

1 package dry yeast, or ½ cup homemade yeast (recipe on page 181)

2 teaspoons sugar or molasses

1 teaspoon salt

6–7 cups flour, measured after sifting

Modern Method:

1. Cook rice in water until soft. Drain excess water, reserving 1 cup if packaged yeast is used. Cool rice and liquid until lukewarm.

2. Dissolve yeast in reserved liquid to which sugar or molasses has been added. If homemade yeast is used, add sugar or molasses.

3. Add rice, salt, and flour, blending to form a soft dough.

4. Knead for 10 minutes. Cover and let rise for 1½–2 hours.

5. Divide dough in half. Place in two ungreased 5-by-9-inch loaf pans or two 8-inch or 9-inch pie plates. Let rise 1 hour.

6. Bake at 350°F for ¾ hour.

Hearth Method:

1. Follow Step 1 in the Modern Method recipe, using a hanging kettle over a moderate fire.

2. Follow Steps 2–5 in the Modern Method recipe.

3. Bake bread in hot brick oven for 45–50 minutes, or use preheated Dutch ovens with coals on lid and below.

Yield: two 8-inch or 9-inch rounds, or two 5-by-9-inch loaves

Rolls

2 tablespoons butter

1 cup milk, at room temperature

1 package yeast, or ½ cup homemade yeast (recipe on page 181)

1 teaspoon salt

4 cups flour

1 teaspoon baking soda

"At dinner parties it is customary to have light French rolls instead of pieces of cut bread. Warm an ounce of butter in half a pint of milk, then add a spoonful and a half of yeast, and a little salt. Put two pounds of flour in a pan, and mix in the above ingredients. Let it rise an hour—or over night in a cool place; knead it well. Make into seven rolls, and bake them in a quick oven. Add half a teaspoonful of saleratus, just as you put the rolls into the baker."

—The New England Economical Housekeeper, 1845

Modern Method:

1. Melt butter. Using a large bowl combine butter, milk, yeast, and salt. Mixture will be foamy.

2. Mix in flour and baking soda. Knead for 10 minutes. Cover bowl and leave to rise in a warm place for about an hour or refrigerate overnight.

3. Shape into four rolled loaves or three-dozen finger rolls. Arrange on a greased cookie sheet, leaving room for rolls to expand. Let rise until doubled in bulk.

4. Bake at 400°F for 20 minutes.

Hearth Method:

1. Melt butter in a large mixing bowl set on a trivet over coals. When butter has melted, remove bowl from fire. Add milk, yeast, and salt. Mixture will be foamy.

2. Follow Step 2 in the Modern Method recipe.

3. Shape dough into four rolled loaves or three-dozen finger rolls, and place on ovenproof pottery or cast-iron baking sheets, leaving room for rolls to expand. Let rise 2 hours or until doubled in bulk.

4. Bake in a hot brick oven or preheated Dutch oven for 20 minutes.

Yield: four loaves or three-dozen finger rolls

Long Rolls

"Take two pounds of flour, rub into it two ounces of butter and two ounces of loaf sugar finely powdered. Put to these four large spoonfuls of pretty thick yeast, and milk enough, made just warm, to mix it into a light paste. Set this before the fire to rise for half an hour, then roll out the dough thin into moderate lengths, let them stand before the fire an hour and bake them in a slack oven for half an hour."

—*The Experienced American Housekeeper,* 1829

2 tablespoons butter

1 tablespoon sugar

5 cups flour

2 cups milk

2 packages yeast dissolved in ¼ cup water

Modern Method:

1. Rub butter and sugar into 4 cups of flour. Warm milk and add to mixture. Stir in dissolved yeast. Mixture will be thick and sticky. Cover bowl with damp cloth and let rise ½ hour. Dough will double in size.

2. Add remaining 1 cup flour to dough and shape into 16 rolls, about by 3 inches by 2 inches in length. Place on greased baking sheets and let rise ½ hour.

3. Bake in preheated 350°F oven for 25–30 minutes.

Hearth Method:

1. To warm milk, set in a shallow bowl on a trivet over hot coals.

2. Follow the rest of Step 1 as in Modern Method recipe.

3. Follow Step 2 of the Modern Method recipe, placing rolls on greased redware plates to rise.

4. Preheat bake-kettle for 15 minutes.

5. Bake in preheated bake-kettle for 25–30 minutes. These rolls may also be baked in a moderate brick oven.

Yield: 16 rolls

Rusks

¼ pound butter

1 cup milk

7 eggs

6 tablespoons sugar

1 package yeast dissolved in ½ cup warm water, or ½ cup homemade yeast (recipe page 181)

6–7 cups flour, wheat and rye, in any proportion

"Beat seven eggs well and mix with half a pint of new milk, in which has been melted four ounces of butter; add to it a quarter of a pint of yeast, and three ounces of sugar and put them, by degrees, into as much flour as will make a very light paste, rather like a batter; and let it rise before the fire half an hour; then add some more flour to make it a little stiffer, but not stiff. Work it well and divide it into small loaves or cakes, about four to six inches wide, and flatten them. When baked and cold, slice them the thickness of rusks, and put them in the oven to brown a little.

"Note. *The cakes, when first baked, eat deliciously buttered for tea; or with caraways to eat cold."*

—*A New System of Domestic Cookery*, 1807

Modern Method:

1. Melt butter and combine with milk.
2. Beat eggs until light; add sugar, yeast, and eggs to milk and butter mixture.
3. Stir in 3 cups of flour and beat for 2–3 minutes. Cover the bowl and set the sponge in a warm place for an hour or more, or refrigerate overnight.
4. To prepare for cooking, add remaining flour so that the dough is no longer sticky.
5. Divide dough in half and make two long rolls. Cut each into twelve slices. Flatten out these slices so that they are 3–4 inches in diameter, resembling an English muffin.
6. Preheat and grease a griddle or heavy skillet. Put three or four cakes on the cooking surface. Cook for 7 minutes, turn, and press down. Cook 7–8 minutes on the other side.
7. Split and serve immediately, with butter and preserves, if desired. After they have cooled, they may be split and toasted. (Use instead of toast for the roasted cheese recipe on page 70.)

Hearth Method:

1. Follow Step 1 in the Modern Method recipe, melt butter in a pan set on a trivet over coals.

2. Follow Steps 2–5 in the Modern Method recipe.

3. Preheat a hanging skillet, grease it, and place three or four cakes on the cooking surface. Cook about 7 minutes, watching that they do not burn. Turn and press down. Cook 7–8 minutes on the other side.

4. Follow Step 7 in the Modern Method recipe.

Yield: 2 dozen

Churn

PRESERVES, &c.

"Economical people will seldom use preserves, except for sickness. They are unhealthy, and useless to those who are well. A pound of sugar to a pound of fruit is the rule for all preserves. The sugar should be melted over a fire moderate enough not to scorch it. When melted, it should be skimmed clean, and the fruit dropped in to simmer till it is soft. Plums and things of which the skin is liable to be broken, do better to be put in little jars, with their weight of sugar and the jars set in a kettle of boiling water till the fruit is done. See the water is not so high as to boil into the jars.

"When you put the preserves in jars, lay a white paper, thoroughly wet with brandy, flat upon the surface of the preserves, and cover them carefully from the air. If they begin to mould, scald them by setting them in the oven till boiling hot. Glass is much better than earthen for preserves: they are not half as apt to ferment."

—*The American Frugal Housewife*, 1832

Pumpkin Preserves

1 sugar pumpkin weighing
3–4 pounds

4–5 cups sugar

2–3 lemons

"Choose a thick yellow pumpkin which is sweet; pare; take out the seeds, and cut the thick part in any form you choose—round, square, egg-shaped, stars, wheels &c.; weigh it; put it in a stone jar or deep dish, and place in a pot of water to boil till the pumpkin is so soft that you can pass a fork through it. The pot may be kept uncovered.

"Take the weight of the pumpkin in good loaf sugar; clarify it and boil the syrup with the juice of one lemon to every pound of sugar, and the peel cut in little squares. When the pumpkin is soft, put it into the syrup and simmer gently about an hour or till the liquor is thick and rich, then let it cool and put it in glass jars well secured from air. It is a very rich sweetmeat."

—*The Good Housekeeper,* 1839

Modern Method:

1. Cut pumpkin in half, scoop out, and discard seeds. Cut along ribs into approximately eight sections. Peel each section and cut away any remaining membrane that supported the seeds.

2. Cut pumpkins into thin strips. Measure pumpkin and add an equal amount of sugar and the juice and peel of one lemon for every 2 cups of pumpkin. Coat pumpkin with sugar-and-lemon mixture. Let the pumpkin mixture sit in a large bowl overnight.

3. Strain off the syrup that has formed in the bowl overnight. Heat the syrup in a double boiler, adding pumpkin slices once the syrup is hot. Heat pumpkin mixture in double boiler for an hour or until tender when pierced with a fork, but not soft. Stir from the bottom several times. Be sure to add water to boiler as needed.

4. Cook preserves until a half-teaspoonful placed on a plate is no longer runny. Pack in sterile glass jars and seal.

Hearth Method:

1. Follow Step 1 and 2 in the Modern Method recipe.

2. Follow Step 3, creating a double boiler by heating hot water in a hanging pot over the fire and placing pumpkin mixture in a stoneware or redware crock until tender when pierced with a fork, but not soft. Stir from the bottom several times. Be sure to add water to the pot as needed. The pumpkin may require up to 2 hours to become tender.

3. Transferring mixture to a tin-lined kettle, follow Step 4 in the Modern Method recipe.

Yield: 4–6 half-pint jars of preserves

Currant Jelly

Freshly picked currants on their stems

Sugar

½ cup brandy

Food-grade paper such as coffee filters

"Currant jelly is a useful thing for sickness. If it be necessary to wash your currants, be sure they are thoroughly drained, or your jelly will be thin. Break them up with a pestle, and squeeze them through a cloth. Put a pint of clean sugar to a pint of juice and boil it slowly, till it becomes ropy. Great care must be taken not to do it too fast; it is spoiled by being scorched. It should be frequently skimmed while simmering. If currants are put in a jar, and kept in boiling water, and cooked before they are strained, they are more likely to keep a long time without fermenting."

—*The American Frugal Housewife*, 1832

Modern and Hearth Methods:

1. Wash currants, put them into a heavy stainless-steel, enameled, or tin-lined pan and heat slowly until liquid forms. Then cook over a higher heat until fruit loses its color.

2. To strain the currants, use a jelly bag made of several thicknesses of cheesecloth. Wet the jelly bag and put the cooked fruit in. Let the liquid drip into a bowl or pan, but do not squeeze the bag, or the jelly will be bitter.

3. Return liquid to heavy cooking pan, and for every cup of juice, add a cup of sugar. Heat slowly to 220°F.

4. Cut circles to the size of the top of the jar from the food-grade paper. Soak circles in brandy.

5. Ladle jelly into sterilized jars. Press brandy-soaked circles on top of hot jelly, pressing gently to remove any air pockets.

Yield: 8 ounces jelly for each cup of juice and cup of sugar

Apple Sauce

"In the country it is thought almost as indispensable to provide the stock of apple sauce for winter use as the pork; and there is no doubt of the healthiness as well as pleasantness of fruit taken in this way as food. To eat with meat, it is best made of sour apples, not too mellow, but pleasant flavored. Boil down new sweet cider till it is nearly as thick, when cold, as molasses; strain it through a sieve; wash the kettle (it must be brass, or iron tinned); put in the syrup, and as soon as it boils, put in the apples, which must have been previously pared, quartered, and cored. Stew over a slow fire of coals till very tender.

"If you like it sweet to eat with tea, use sweet apples and skim out the whole quarters, when soft; then boil the syrup and pour over them."

—*The Good Housekeeper,* 1839

3 pounds apples

½ gallon cider

Modern Method:

1. The day before: Peel the apples, remove core, and cut into quarters. Set aside to partially dehydrate. Do not cover with plastic wrap.
2. Simmer cider until reduced by half and syrupy.
3. Stew apples in reduced cider until just tender.
4. Serve applesauce by itself, or use in the recipe for Apple Pie on page 144.

Hearth Method:

1. Follow Step 1 in the Modern Method recipe
2. Follow Steps 2–4 in the Modern Method recipe, using a large hanging pot.

Yield: 2 quarts

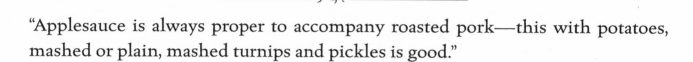

"Applesauce is always proper to accompany roasted pork—this with potatoes, mashed or plain, mashed turnips and pickles is good."

—Sarah J. Hale, *The Way to Live Well and Be Well While We Live*
(Philadelphia, 1847)

Cranberry Sauce

"Wash a quart of ripe cranberries, and put them into a pan with about a wine-glass of water. Stew them slowly, and stir them frequently, particularly after they begin to burst. They require a great deal of stewing, and should be like a marmalade when done. After you take them from the fire, stir in a pound of brown sugar. You may strain the pulp through a cullendar or sieve into a mould, and when it is in a firm shape send it to table on a glass dish."
—*Directions for Cookery, 1851*

1 pound cranberries

2–3 cups sweetening, sugar or molasses or a combination

Modern Method:

1. Simmer cranberries over low heat, until soft, approximately 12–15 minutes.
2. Straining is optional. To remove seeds and skins, use a food mill or strain pulp through a very coarse strainer. Reheat before adding sugar or molasses. Use only about 2 cups of sugar or molasses if skins and seeds have been discarded.
3. Stir sugar or molasses into hot sauce and remove from heat when completely melted, about 2–3 minutes. Serve hot or cold.

Hearth Method:

1. Follow Step 1 in the Modern Method recipe, using a large hanging kettle over a slow fire or a redware bowl on a trivet over hot coals.
2. Follow Steps 2 and 3 in the Modern Method recipe.

Yield: 6 cups

Catsup

Tomatoes

Salt

Whole cloves

Whole allspice berries

Mace

Pepper

Garlic

Mustard seed

"The best sort of catsup is made from tomatoes. The vegetables should be squeezed up in the hand, salt put to them, and set by for twenty-four hours. After being passed through a sieve, cloves, allspice, pepper, mace, garlic, and whole mustard-seed should be added. It should be boiled down one third, and bottled after it is cool. No liquid is necessary, as the tomatoes are very juicy. A good deal of salt and spice is necessary to keep the catsup well. It is delicious with roast meat; and a cupful adds much to the richness of soup and chowder. The garlic should be taken out before it is bottled."

—*The American Frugal Housewife,* 1832

Modern Method:

1. Chop and crush fresh, ripe tomatoes. For every 4 good-sized tomatoes, sprinkle 2 tablespoons of salt. Cover and refrigerate for 24 hours.
2. Puree tomatoes in a blender or food mill and measure.
3. To each quart of puree, add 4 whole cloves, 4 whole allspice berries, 1/8 teaspoon mace, 1 teaspoon pepper, 1 garlic clove, and 1/2 teaspoon mustard seed.
4. Simmer slowly in a pan to blend flavors and reduce by one-third to one-half. This will take approximately 2–2½ hours, depending on the quantity and kind of tomatoes used and the type of pan. (It will take less time if an uncovered electric skillet is used.) The catsup will be brown and is ready when the liquid has boiled away. Remove garlic before packing in sterilized pint jars. Seal according to manufacturer's directions.

Hearth Method:

Follow Steps 1–4 in the Modern Method recipe, using a tin-lined pan to reduce the ingredients.

Yield: 1 pint per 4 large tomatoes

Horseradish Cream

"Mix a tea-spoonful of mustard, a table-spoonful of vinegar, and three of cream; add a little salt, and as much finely-grated horse-radish as will make the sauce the consistence of onion sauce."

—The Practice of Cookery, 1830

5–ounce jar prepared horseradish

5 tablespoons vinegar

3 tablespoons cream

2 teaspoons prepared mustard

2 tablespoons sugar

Modern and Hearth Methods:

Mix all ingredients together.

Yield: ¾ cup relish

Pickling to Preserve Vegetables

Brine (6 tablespoons salt to a quart of water)

1 quart vinegar

2 tablespoons whole peppercorns

1 tablespoon whole allspice

1 tablespoon whole mustard seed

Cucumbers, washed and packed in large jar; or red cabbage, washed, shredded, and packed in large jar; or green tomatoes, washed and packed in large jar

"Cucumbers should be in weak brine three or four days after they are picked; then they should be put in a tin or wooden pail of clean water, and kept slightly warm in the kitchen corner for two or three days. Then take as much vinegar as you think your pickle jar will hold; scald it with pepper, allspice, mustard-seed, flagroot, horseradish, &c., if you happen to have them; half of them will spice the pickles very well. Throw in a bit of alum as big as a walnut; this serves to make pickles hard. Skim the vinegar clean, and pour it scalding hot upon the cucumbers. Brass vessels are not healthy for preparing anything acid. Red cabbages need no other pickling than scalding, spiced vinegar poured upon them, and suffered to remain eight or ten days before you eat them. Some people think it improves them to keep them in salt and water twenty-four hours before they are pickled."

—The American Frugal Housewife, 1832

Modern and Hearth Methods:

1. Make brine to soak cucumbers overnight.
2. In morning, simmer vinegar with spices for 10 minutes in a stainless-steel or enameled pot.
3. Drain brine from cucumbers. Pour vinegar immediately over the cucumbers, cabbage, or tomatoes, packed in stoneware, lead-free pottery, or glass jars. Vinegar solution must completely cover vegetables.
4. Cover and let set a week or so in a cool place before eating.

Yield: 1 gallon

The American Citron

"Take the rind of a large watermelon not too ripe, cut it into small pieces. Take two pounds of loaf sugar; one pint of water and put it all into a kettle, let it boil gently for four hours, then put it into pots for use."

—*The American Frugal Housewife,* 1832

1 small round watermelon or ⅓ of a very large oval watermelon

4 cups sugar

2 cups water

Modern Method:

1. Chop watermelon rind into ½-inch cubes.

2. Place rinds, sugar, and water in a large heavy pan. Bring to a boil, then turn down heat and simmer 3–4 hours until rind is tender and a thick syrup has formed.

3. If not to be used immediately, pack in sterilized pint jars and seal according to manufacturer's directions.

4. Use in the recipe for Wedding Cake on page 162 or for other fruitcakes, or serve as relish.

Hearth Method:

1. Follow Steps 1 and 2 in the Modern Method recipe, using a small tin-lined or enameled hanging kettle over a slow fire.

2. Follow Steps 3 and 4 in the Modern Method recipe.

Yield: 3–4 pints

Pumpkin Leather

1 pumpkin

"Some people cut pumpkin, string it and dry it like apples. It is much better way to boil and sift the pumpkin, then spread it out thin in tin plates, and dry hard in a warm oven. It will keep good all the year round and a little piece boiled up in milk will make a batch of pies."

--The American Frugal Housewife, 1832

Modern Method:

1. Boil pumpkin (or squash) until soft.
2. Push flesh through fine sieve.
3. Spread pumpkin puree on lightly greased jelly-roll type baking sheet about ½ inch thick.
4. Place in 150°F oven. Stick wooden spoon in door of oven to keep it open a crack. Leave several hours or overnight.
5. As long as it is dried completely, the pumpkin leather can be stored in any type of airtight container.

Hearth Method:

1. Follow Step 1 in the Modern Method recipe, hanging kettle over fire.
2. Follow Steps 2 and 3.
3. Place in bake-oven after all other baking is done. Leave in overnight.

To Use Pumpkin Leather:

Soak 1 cup of dried pumpkin overnight in milk. In the morning, simmer pumpkin until it absorbs milk and rehydrates. It can also be rehydrated in water and added to soups or stews. Use in the recipe for Pumpkin Pie on page 138 or Indian Cake on page 171, or any other recipe calling for pumpkin.

Kitchen Pepper

"Mix in the finest powder, one ounce of ginger, of cinnamon, black pepper, nutmeg, and Jamaica pepper, half an ounce of each, ten cloves and six ounces of salt. Keep it in a bottle— it is an agreeable addition to any brown sauces or soups.

"Spice in powder, kept in small bottles close stopped, goes much further than when used whole. It must be dried before pounded; and should be done in quantities that may be wanted in three or four months. Nutmeg need not be done—but the others should be kept in separate bottle with a little label on each."

—*A New System of Domestic Cookery,* 1807

Modern and Hearth Methods:

1. Mix ingredients together
2. Store in tightly sealed jar or bottle. Use to flavor soups, stews, and roasts.

Yield: ½ cup

2 tablespoons ground ginger

2 teaspoons ground cinnamon

2 teaspoons ground black pepper

2 teaspoons ground nutmeg

2 teaspoons ground allspice

½ teaspoon ground cloves

4 tablespoon salt

Excellent Lemonade

2 quarts water

Juice of 5 lemons

Grated rind of 3 lemons

1 cup sugar

"Take good lemons, roll them; then cut and squeeze them into a pitcher. Add loaf sugar and cold water, till it makes a pleasant drink. It should be sweet; it is sometimes too acid to be agreeable. Send round in small glasses with handles, or tumblers a little more than half full. The best drink for parties."

—The Skilful Housewife, 1846

Modern and Hearth Methods:
1. Mix ingredients together.
2. Strain and chill.

Yield: 4 servings

Raspberry Shrub

"Raspberry shrub mixed with water is a pure, delicious drink for summer; and in a country where raspberries are abundant, it is good economy to make it answer instead of Port and Catalonia wine. Put raspberries in a pan, and scarcely cover them with strong vinegar. Add a pint of sugar to a pint of juice (of this you can judge by first trying your pan to see how much it holds); scald it, skim it, and bottle it when cold."

—*The American Frugal Housewife*, 1832

Raspberries

Vinegar

Sugar

Note: Shrub is a method of preserving small fruits such as currants or raspberries by producing a syrup from the fruit juice and sugar. The word *shrub* comes from the Arabic *sharb*, meaning "drink." Shrub was traditionally made with orange or lemon juice, sugar, and rum, but the temperance movement of the nineteenth century saw vinegar substituted for the rum, with a qualifying word to indicate the type of small fruit used.

Modern and Hearth Methods:

1. Cover raspberries with vinegar in a kettle. Do not use cast iron.
2. Simmer until berries are soft.
3. Strain through cheesecloth. Measure juice.
4. For each cup of juice, add 1 cup of sugar.
5. Bring juice and sugar just to a boil, skim the top, and ladle into sterilized glass jars. Keep cold or seal jars to store.
6. To serve, mix shrub with water to taste.

Coffee

"Put two ounces of fresh-ground coffee, of the best quality, into a coffee-pot, and pour eight coffee-cups of boiling water on it; let it boil six minutes; pour out a cupful two or three times, and return it again; then put two or three isinglass-chips into it, and pour one large spoonful of boiling water on it; boil it five minutes more, and set the pot by the fire to keep hot for ten minutes, and you will have coffee of a beautiful clearness.

"Fine cream should always be served with coffee, and either pounded sugar-candy, or fine sugar."

—*A New System of Domestic Cookery,* 1807

Modern Method:

1. Roast coffee beans in an ungreased roaster or iron skillet over low heat, stirring frequently until they are dark and brittle.
2. Keep roasted beans in a tightly covered container. Grind coffee before using.

Hearth Method:

1. Follow Step 1 in Modern Method recipe using a hanging skillet or metal pan on a trivet over hot coals.
2. Follow Step 2 in the Modern Method recipe.

Modern Method:

1. Use a saucepan and put in 1–2 tablespoons ground coffee to every 2 cups boiling water. Drop in egg white and washed eggshell.

2. Bring to boil and simmer 20 minutes.

3. Let coffee stand 5 minutes before straining into pot for serving.

Hearth Method:

1. Follow Step 1 in the Modern Method recipe, using a tin coffee pot.

2. Put pot on a trivet over hot coals to boil for 20–25 minutes.

3. Follow Step 3 in the Modern Method recipe.

TO BREW COFFEE:
Ground coffee

Water

Egg white

½ eggshell, crushed

Coffee Grinder

Chocolate

1 ounce unsweetened chocolate, grated

¼ cup sugar

½ teaspoon ground nutmeg, optional

2 cups water

2 cups milk

"Many people boil chocolate in a coffee-pot; but I think it is better to boil it in a skillet, or something open. A piece of chocolate about as big as a dollar is the usual quantity for a quart of water; but some put in more, and some less. When it boils, pour in as much milk as you like, and let them boil together three or four minutes. It is much richer with the milk boiled into it. Put the sugar in either before or after, as you please. Nutmeg improves it. The chocolate should be scraped fine before it is put into the water."

—*The American Frugal Housewife*, 1832

Modern Method:

1. Melt chocolate in a double boiler. Add sugar and nutmeg, if desired, and stir.
2. Add water, and bring to a boil.
3. Add milk, and heat to serving temperature, about 3–4 minutes.
4. Serve hot with grated nutmeg.

Hearth Method:

1. Follow Step 1 in the Modern Method recipe, using a skillet over a slow fire.
2. Follow Steps 2–4 in the Modern Method recipe.

Yield: 4 servings

Harvest Drink

"Mix with five gallons of good water, half a gallon of molasses, one quart of vinegar and two ounces of powdered ginger. This will make not only a very pleasant beverage, but one highly invigorating and healthful."

—The Skilful Housewife, 1846

½ gallon water

1½ cups molasses

¾ cup cider vinegar

2 teaspoon powdered ginger

Note: Harvest Drink is often referred to as Haymaker's Switchel, since many New England farmers made this thirst-quenching concoction to bring to the field to refresh them while cutting hay. As with Shrub, this recipe for switchel by the nineteenth century was influenced by the growing temperance movement, and no longer included rum as a vital ingredient. Switchel was viewed as "highly invigorating" and "healthful," with the ingredients designed not only to stop dehydration but also to satisfy the thirst.

Modern and Hearth Method:
Mix ingredients together. May be chilled, but is refreshing at room temperature as well.

Yield: 6 servings

Sources of the Recipes

Abell, Mrs. L. G. *The Skilful Housewife's Book, or Complete Guide to Domestic Cookery, Taste, Comfort, and Economy.* New York: D. Newell, 1846.

Buist, Robert. *Family Kitchen Gardener.* New York: O. Judd, 1847.

Child, Lydia Maria. *The American Frugal Housewife Dedicated to Those Who Are Not Ashamed of Economy.* 12th ed. Boston: Carter, Hendee, and Co., 1832.

Dalgairns, Mrs. *The Practice of Cookery, Adapted to the Business of Everyday Life.* Boston: Munroe and Francis, 1830.

Emerson, Lucy, comp. *The New England Cookery.* Montpelier, Vt.: Joseph Parks, 1808.

Green, Francis H. *The Housekeeper's Book.* Philadelphia: W. Marshall & Co., 1838.

Hale, Sarah Josepha. *The Good Housekeeper: The Way to Live Well and Be Well While We Live*, 2nd ed. Boston: Weeks, Jordan & Co., 1839.

——. *The Ladies' New Book of Cookery: Practical System for Private Families in Town and Country.* New York: H. Long & Brothers, 1852.

Howland, Mrs. E. A. *The New England Economical Housekeeper.* Worcester, Mass.: S. A. Howland, 1845.

Kitchener, William. *The Cook's Oracle.* Boston: Munroe and Francis, 1823.

Lee, Mrs. N. K. M. *The Cook's Own Book.* Boston: Munroe and Francis, 1832.

Leslie, Eliza. *Directions for Cookery.* Philadelphia: Henry Carey Baird, 1851.

——. *Seventy-Five Receipts For Pastry, Cakes And Sweetmeats.* Boston: Munroe and Francis, 1830.

Mrs. Gardiner's Receipts from 1763. Hallowell, Maine: White & Horne, 1938. [Manuscript recipes of 1763.]

Roberts, Robert. *The House Servant's Directory, or Monitor for Private Families.* Boston: Munroe and Francis, 1827 (1977 facsimile ed. Gore Place, Waltham, Mass.).

Rundell, Maria Eliza Ketelby. *A New System of Domestic Cookery*, Boston: W. Andrews, 1807.

——. *The Experienced American Housekeeper or Domestic Cookery*. Hartford: Silas Andrus, 1829.

Simmons, Amelia. *American Cookery*. 2nd ed. Brattleboro, Vt.: William Fessenden, 1814. [A facsimile of the first edition, published in 1796 has most recently been reprinted by Applewood Press in 1996.]

Metric Conversion Tables

Approximate U.S.–Metric Equivalents

Liquid Ingredients

U.S. MEASURES	METRIC	U.S. MEASURES	METRIC
¼ TSP.	1.23 ML	2 TBSP.	29.57 ML
½ TSP.	2.36 ML	3 TBSP.	44.36 ML
¾ TSP.	3.70 ML	¼ CUP	59.15 ML
1 TSP.	4.93 ML	½ CUP	118.30 ML
1¼ TSP.	6.16 ML	1 CUP	236.59 ML
1½ TSP.	7.39 ML	2 CUPS OR 1 PT.	473.18 ML
1¾ TSP.	8.63 ML	3 CUPS	709.77 ML
2 TSP.	9.86 ML	4 CUPS OR 1 QT.	946.36 ML
1 TBSP.	14.79 ML	4 QTS. OR 1 GAL.	3.79 LT

Dry Ingredients

U.S. MEASURES		METRIC	U.S. MEASURES	METRIC
17⅗ OZ.	1 LIVRE	500 G	2 OZ.	60 (56.6) G
16 OZ.	1 LB.	454 G	1¾ OZ.	50 G
8⅞ OZ.		250 G	1 OZ.	30 (28.3) G
5¼ OZ.		150 G	⅞ OZ.	25 G
4½ OZ.		125 G	¾ OZ.	21 (21.3) G
4 OZ.		115 (113.2) G	½ OZ.	15 (14.2) G
3½ OZ.		100 G	¼ OZ.	7 (7.1) G
3 OZ.		85 (84.9) G	⅛ OZ.	3½ (3.5) G
2⅘ OZ.		80 G	1/16 OZ.	2 (1.8) G

Index